Dedication

Dedicated with love and admiration to my son, Brandon, who has taught me how to view life differently while seeing the world through his eyes and watching him bravely maneuver through the days with his fierce determination. Brandon continues to be my finest teacher.

To my son, Matthew, for all his love and support on this project and in everyday life. I treasure all the joy and laughter we've shared over the years. I know that I can count on you to be there through thick and thin, and that's priceless.

And to all the courageous and loving parents who are on the same path as I am, who are seeking to gain freedom and independence for their autistic and special needs children, and to ensure they are well taken care of and never forgotten.

Acknowledgments

I am forever grateful to my wonderful family and friends Matthew, Trisha, Sydney, Reed, Dede, Gina, Eileen, Kenny, Lora, Jane, Maggie and Lane who have offered to step in and help and support Brandon after I'm gone. You have all given me the greatest gift one could give a mother. Because of your compassion and generosity, I will be able to leave the planet in peace when the time comes.

In appreciation to Rory Patton, Christopher A. Poulos, Mary Anne Ehlert, Bart Stevens and Rick Benzel for your invaluable contributions to this manuscript; to reader Lora Mancini for all your wonderful feedback and support, and to Helen Milner who enthusiastically offered to do the final read through, and to my dear friend, Dede Utzinger, copy editor extraordinaire.

I especially want to thank my tireless editor and loyal friend, Stephanie Vitale, who has journeyed with me through the writing of this, as well as my first book, *Raising Brandon*, and without whom neither book would have been possible.

Praise for *I Have Autism…What'll I Do Without You, Mom?*

"Amalia is a Pioneer in the Autism Community. As Amalia provides practical advice on tackling the tough issues of parenting, you are swept away by the continuing saga of her life as a special needs mom. Every parent wants to make sure their child has the opportunity to live their life fully and with as much independence as possible. We all want to ensure that our children can live on their own after we're gone. Amalia's book is an easy-to-read manual which gives parents practical tools to get them started on the right track."
- *Joel Manzer, Lead Editor,* Autisable.com

"I couldn't think or talk about my own mortality even though I knew I should. Thank you for writing this book and making it easier for me to face this very important subject."
- *Sharon Fitzgerald, Parent, California*

"Amalia Starr gives parents courage and hope to face the anxieties and realities of independence for our growing population of young adults with Autism."
- *Marianne Russo, President,* The Coffee Klatch Special Needs Talk Radio Network

"I never thought I could leave my disabled son without me. But now I feel if I make a plan I may be able to go in peace."
- *Bill Davies, Parent, New Jersey*

"This is a very important book and well written with the sensitivity of a loving mother. Death and dying is something we must all talk about, especially when we have a child with special needs."
- *Catherine Wallace, Social Worker, Florida*

"After reading your book and learning what to do about my daughter's future I have much less fear. Thank you!"
- *Lucinda Hunt, Parent, Iowa*

"Amalia has truly helped me and my family stay on track for improving life for my thirty-five-year-old autistic brother. Her inspiration and knowledge have lit a fire within me for improving his conditions and securing a good future for him. She has provided me with concrete ideas, tips and solutions on how to reach this goal."
- *Kristoffer Hanson, Brother, Sweden*

I Have Autism...
What'll I Do Without You, Mom?

How to Prepare for When Your Special Needs Child Outlives You

Amalia Starr

Mountain Star Publishing

Mountain Star Publishing
P.O. Box 1357
Sierra Madre, CA 91025
mountainstarpublishing@gmail.com

I Have Autism…What'll I Do Without You, Mom? How to Prepare for When Your Special Needs Child Outlives You
Copyright © October 2014 by Amalia Starr.

All rights reserved. No part of this book may be reproduced or transmitted by any form or by any means, electronic, or mechanical, including photocopying, recording or by any information storage and retrieval system without written permission from the publisher, except for the inclusion of a brief quotation in a review.

Library of Congress Control Number: 2014902796
Mountain Star Publishing

Starr, Amalia (2014)
I have autism…what'll i do without you, mom? how to prepare for when your special needs child outlives you
1. Parenting. 2. Autism. 3. Epilepsy. 4. Special Needs. 5. Disabilities. 6. Independence.
I. Title.
ISBN: 0982137796
ISBN 13: 978-0-9821377-9-6

Editor: Stephanie R. Vitale

Printed in the United States of America

Contents

Introduction 1
SECTION ONE: YOU ARE NOT ALONE: 5
1. Parenting in the Dark 7
2. How to Help Your Child Succeed 11
3. The Natural Progression of Life 19

SECTION TWO: TAKE ACTION: 23
4. How to Create Your Personalized
   Instructional Care Manual 25
   Sample Instructional Care Manual 33
5. How to Set Up Your Step-In Parenting Network 59

SECTION THREE: HELPFUL STORIES AND ANSWERS: 81
6. Teaching Stories and Questions & Answers 83

SECTION FOUR: INDEPENDENCE: 109
7. How to Prepare You and Your
   Child for Independence 111
8. You Need to Have a Plan 129

SECTION FIVE: LEGAL MATTERS: 159
9. Financial Planning and Legal Matters
   Wills, Guardianship and Much More 161

Epilogue 179
Appendix 183
About the Author 189
Your Working Instructional Care Manual 191
The Final Instructional Care Manual 233

Introduction

"I don't know what I would do without you, Mom."

Brandon

Several years ago my son, Brandon, had yet another epileptic seizure and was taken to the hospital. He has had them often, but this time he was unable to walk afterwards. He could not even touch his foot to the ground. When he was released from the hospital, he somehow got himself into a cab and went home. He called me and left a voice mail to tell me about the incident.

I was just returning from a speaking engagement. After I got off the plane, I called Brandon, reassuring him that I was on my way to help. He told me, "No Mom, don't come. I just need to sleep." Sleep can be very healing after having a seizure, so I told him to call me when he woke up.

The following morning he wasn't feeling better, so I went over and convinced him to go to his holistic practitioner for a treatment. She knows how to balance Brandon's body after he has a seizure. I helped my thirty-eight year old, six-foot-two autistic son out of his apartment and drove him to his practitioner's office. After the treatment he was able to walk somewhat on his own although he was still in pain and very wobbly. Brandon said that he was feeling better and admitted he was glad he went for the treatment. He asked if I could do his marketing for him before I took him home. We drove to the store where I left him in the car while I shopped. I wanted him to have whatever he needed while he spent the next several days in his apartment recuperating.

After arriving home, Brandon immediately went to lie down on his bed. As he watched me bring in the last bag of groceries, he said, "I don't know what I would do without you, Mom." It felt wonderful to hear those words, but at the same I was deeply saddened; I couldn't help but wonder what the future held for my son. The minute I said goodbye and closed the door behind me, tears began to leak from my eyes. On the hour ride home I cried like a baby. "What will Brandon do after I'm gone?" I thought. At that very moment I knew what I had to do.

If you are a parent of a special needs child you will understand what this book is about. One of your biggest fears is that your child will outlive you and there will be no one around to care for your son or daughter as well as you can. This frightening unknown haunts parents daily because they believe it is out of their control.

How would you feel if I told you there are things you can do right now to help you sleep better at night? *How comforting would it be for you to know you can help your adult child live well after you are gone?* I believe this knowledge would be a great relief to you—and that is why I wrote this book.

I have created a comprehensive, step-by-step plan and a personalized Instructional Care Manual for you to complete so that others can take care of and help your child live well. I will show you how to find the right people "to stand in for you" by creating a network of supportive individuals who can assist and be an advocate for your child. My Step-In Parenting Network program (SIPN) will help you identify potential "step-in parents" who can continue to love and care for your child when you no longer can.

I've also included detailed chapters on independence because what you do today to help your child reach maximum independence will affect the quality of the rest of his or her life. Working on "letting go" of a special needs adult child is a sensitive area that many parents are afraid to face head on. However, the more your child knows and can learn to do, one step at a time, the easier it will be for your son or daughter to continue on.

We cannot pretend that our children will magically be taken care of in the future if we don't do something about it today. This is why the Instructional

Care Manual (ICM) will be crucial for every child with special needs. *It will follow them everywhere they go for the rest of their lives.*

I wrote this book to inspire you to move forward, knowing that there are things you can do to ensure that your child is not alone or forgotten. By taking action now, you will feel as empowered and relieved as I have become, through the Step-In Parenting Network program and the Instructional Care Manual I created. This book is your best opportunity to be heard and to help your adult child reach maximum independence and live the best life possible—while you are still here, and after you're gone.

Before You Begin

A Few Words of Encouragement

I have spent the past four years writing this book because I knew how very important it was to talk about this subject. As tough as it is, it is a necessity for all special needs parents to face the future one step, one day, one page at a time. This book was written to bring you Hope, Courage, Information, Support and Comfort. You can begin on any page and at your own pace. I want to encourage you to write in this book and get your information and feelings written down on paper. I believe you will find it to be very healing. I am here to cheer you on and hold your hand as we walk together along this path for the good of our children and for our own peace of mind.

Let's get started!

SECTION ONE

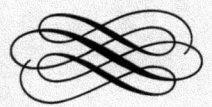

You Are Not Alone

I Walk This Journey With You

One

Parenting in the Dark

Only in darkness can you see the stars.

Dr. Martin Luther King, Jr.

My oldest son, Matt, was born in 1970. He was adorable, sweet, and easy to parent. Two years later my second son, Brandon, was born and my life changed completely. It literally began to fall apart. He had autism, epilepsy, and severe learning disorders, although it took years to find this out.

Those first few years while raising Brandon I often found myself stuck in shame, frozen with fear and paralyzed by pride. My son took forever to learn to speak so others could understand him; he reacted strangely to sounds and light; he seldom expressed an emotion other than crying, which he did quite often. I knew something was different about him but I didn't know what. It was 1973 and no one understood why he acted the way he did. I was "parenting in the dark."

I had many private "Why me?" pity parties and I shed many tears. I made a sign that said "Unfair" and would march around the house with it when no one was home shouting, "UNFAIR! UNFAIR!" I was sad, frustrated and angry and I had no one to talk to. I often lived in the future—what I called the "what if" zone. I asked myself dozens of "what if" questions, which only made me more anxious and fearful.

When Brandon began kindergarten, he could not make a friend, although he never stopped trying. Words would fly out of his mouth backwards and all mixed up, and what he said often irritated the other children. He became a target of ridicule. In elementary school he was beaten up and bullied several times a week and the teachers did nothing about it.

In 1982, at nine, Brandon had his first seizure. The neurologist told us he had epilepsy. She strongly advised we keep it a secret due to the stigma attached to those who suffered from it. But of course, keeping a health issue of this magnitude a secret created far more harm than good and only served to heap shame on an already alarming diagnosis.

You might need to sit down for this next comment. The missing piece of the puzzle—learning that Brandon had autism—did not come out until he was *thirty-two years old*. I can only imagine what my life would have been like if I had known about this decades ago, and I can only imagine what Brandon's life would have been like if he had been diagnosed sooner and we had the knowledge and plans that I am about to impart to you.

Acceptance

Most parents raising a special needs child have felt pain, sadness, resentment, despair, loss, and every other emotion in between. However, it is a necessary process to learn how to move through these feelings, and especially how to let them go.

I could not rid myself of my negative feelings until I was able to accept Brandon for exactly who he was. It took me many years before I was able to even *begin* to let go of these crippling feelings. What I have learned is that the sooner you are able to accept your child and recognize that your son or daughter is not your opponent and that you are on the same team, raising your child will become much easier.

What I wish someone would have told me years ago is that we need to be kind to ourselves. We need to take care of ourselves first. We must be able to ask for help and support from people who care. The great news is that today you don't have to do this alone.

As parents of a special needs child, you are asked to navigate along a very winding, bumpy road with many unexpected twists and turns. It takes stamina and perseverance. But you do it because you love your child. You want your child to live the best life possible, which is every parent's dream.

If you have been told that when your child reaches a certain age he or she will not continue to grow and develop, or that your child will never be able to do something, I suggest you take it with a grain of salt. I have heard this from many professionals over the years and several of my clients were told the same. No one really knows what the future brings and it is much more constructive to focus on and cultivate what can be done, rather than on what cannot.

Independence is a Process

Independence is a step-by-step lifelong process. I have found with Brandon at age forty that I still continue to teach him, but most often from a distance and by being an example. I will go into further detail about achieving independence in Chapters Seven and Eight. This is an area parents have great difficulty with, especially when it comes to moving through their fears and actually "letting go" of their adult special needs child.

Helping Brandon grow up to be an adult has given me a second chance in life and the opportunity to become a kinder, more loving mother. He has given me the strength to discard or change my unwanted patterns and behaviors. He has taught me the true meaning of life, how to let go of negativity and to focus on what is important—the here and now, this very moment. Today, we have a very rich and deep connection. We understand one another, even when no words are spoken.

I am a firm believer that the first step for any parent of a special needs child is to help that child become as independent as possible. There is an enormous range of what independence means, so please take this in the largest context possible, and know that it comes from my heart. I know that every child is a unique individual and the level of independence that can be achieved will reflect the child's own limitations and strengths. In my view, the overriding principle for parents is to try to help their child learn to become as self-reliant as possible, to whatever degree that is.

Frankly, I learned this from Brandon, and it is one of many lessons he has taught me. My son was always very determined, and when he wanted something he got it. You have to admit that this is a fabulous trait to have. There has not been very much that Brandon has wanted over the years, but once he made it clear that living with me or with strangers was out of the question, the case was *closed.*

It is natural to be fearful and worried about what will happen to our kids when they become adults. We must dig deep, very deep, and learn to trust ourselves and our child, and to be courageous, more courageous than we ever thought possible. There were many times I would ask myself if I was making a big mistake allowing my son to pursue his dream of living on his own. But over time, as I saw him continue to make progress and grow, I came to realize it was a good decision. Brandon celebrated seventeen years of independence in 2014. His successes have given me the courage to stay the course.

Brandon simplifies his life by focusing on the moment. He does not carry old baggage from one day into the next. He has great difficulty with everyday tasks such as making his bed or opening cans or bottles, which are nearly impossible due to his lack of fine and gross motor skills. Because he has intractable epilepsy he will never be able to drive a car, so he must rely on walking and public transportation to get where he is going.

Brandon is a kind and gentle man, but he is quite naïve and is not able to express himself well. Many who don't know him think he is rude or weird and he is often misunderstood. Consequently, he has few friends.

His life is far from perfect and never will be. Almost every day there are challenges he must face. My goal is to continue to teach my son so that he will be able to live independently after I am gone. I will support, guide and love him until the day I leave the planet. However, I will continue to step further back and let go more and more each day to allow him the space to become even more independent.

Two

How to Help Your Child Succeed

Once you choose hope, anything's possible.

Christopher Reeve

Last year, I was working with a client whose autistic son was eighteen-years old. She asked me if I had any advice to give to her about what she could do to help her son become more independent and make sure he would be okay after she passed away. I told her that while we are still on the planet we have opportunities that many of us parents miss. I was referring our day-to-day interactions with our special needs children. Below I have written what I mean by "day-to-day interactions" and how you can begin to implement these simple techniques today.

Teach Not Preach

Every time you are with your child you have the opportunity to teach or preach. There is a huge difference between them. Teaching is a positive approach that helps your child grow by suggesting and gently guiding; preaching is an "I told you so" or "You should do it this way" approach that quickly turns negative.

Over the past several years, I have made a conscious effort whenever I am out with Brandon to teach him whatever I could from my heart *first* and *then* from my head. I want him to learn as much as he can while I am still here. I approach this in a fun way. I find he responds well to this type of guidance, given that he is already a middle-aged man and deserves to be treated as an adult, with kindness and respect.

In the last few years I've been able to come alongside Brandon and help him accomplish many tasks that I never thought he would be capable of doing on his own. What takes most of us a few minutes to accomplish would usually take him hours, and what takes us hours would take him days, if he could manage the task at all. I am talking about the things one needs to know and be able to handle to live independently, such as grocery shopping, obtaining a needed service (a phone, for example), changing an address at the post office or ordering a prescription at the pharmacy. If Brandon goes with me on an errand as an observer, I will explain the steps I am taking to accomplish the task; if it is a task he is learning to do for himself and he asks for help, I will gently guide him through the process. My feeling is that whatever my son can pick up from sharing these experiences with me, the better it will be for him now and in the future.

Fun Storytelling

During our conversations I indirectly share different ways to do things, often by storytelling. These stories have become an integral part of our conversations. I make sure I am upbeat, non-judgmental and am using a pleasant tone of voice. Brandon enjoys hearing these stories because he knows he is not alone and that other people are coping with similar difficulties.

One of Brandon's independent living counselors continued to change her appointment times with him. It was hard for Brandon to adjust to this and he told me he didn't like it. I told him I believed that people who make appointments with us should be courteous and respectful of our time. I simply and gently explained that when someone does something we don't like it is important that we tell them.

It took some time for these teaching moments to feel "natural" and to be easily blended into our conversations, but the results have been wonderful. Brandon is like a sponge and has soaked up many important lessons this way. My intention is to teach my son as much as I can whenever we are together. The more he knows the better he will be able to survive and even thrive.

Focus on the Positive

I will share with you another tool that saved my life and Brandon's, too. Out of necessity I made up a game to keep my sanity while raising him. Keep in mind I did not know that Brandon had autism until he was thirty-two years of age. I had no idea what I was dealing with, and as I said earlier, I was parenting in the dark for all those years.

When I wanted to get myself out of a pessimistic mode and into a more cheerful one, *I forced myself to look for something positive in every negative situation.* At the beginning it was extremely difficult to do, so I called it a "game" to try and make it more fun. I stayed with it until I could master it and eventually I was able to completely change my pessimism into optimism at will. I continue to use it successfully in all areas of my life today. Let me give you an example.

Plans Made in Stone

On my way to take Brandon out for dinner I stopped at an ATM machine to get cash. My card got stuck in the machine and I left without my card and without the cash. The restaurant he wanted to go to did not accept credit cards or checks. When I arrived at Brandon's house I asked him if I could borrow $10.00 to take him to dinner and pay him back by check. He quickly shouted, "No!" I tried to explain what had happened and that it would only be a temporary loan until he got to the bank the next day to cash my check. Again he shouted, "No!" I realized that he just did not understand what I was trying to do by borrowing the money. He gets uptight and anxious when it comes to money, as some of us do.

I looked through my wallet and glove compartment and came up with all the money I could find. It added up to $9.43, but I just knew that it would not be enough. I came to visit my son and to have a good time, so to salvage the situation I truly had to find something good in it. Believe me, at that very moment it felt impossible.

I decided I would let him order dinner and I would eat later. It was the perfect solution, as changing to a different, cheaper restaurant at the last minute would have sent Brandon into a tizzy.

On the way to the restaurant I took some deep breaths, got hold of myself, and realized that everything would work out *just fine.* As we were walking to the restaurant Brandon found a crumpled up ten-dollar bill on the sidewalk. You would have thought he had found a million dollars! We both began to laugh. "Mom, I *knew* it would work out!" he exclaimed. Of course, just applying positive thinking will not always bring you money, but it will help bring you peace of mind, which is something money cannot buy.

Allow and Encourage Your Children to Do What They Can Do For Themselves

Too many of us do not have time to allow our children to do things for themselves. For an example, we are often rushing off to appointments and instead of giving our children time to tie their shoes we quickly tie them for them. This type of assistance does not stop here. It actually seems to escalate. I know what it was like for me when Brandon was growing up. I remember when my oldest son, Matthew, said, "Mom, it's not fair that Brandon doesn't have to do chores around the house like the rest of us." He was right, but often when Brandon did chores, it made more work for me. For example, one day I asked him to put away the towels in the linen closet, which I soon discovered he had stuffed in the closet every which way. When I opened the door all the towels fell on the floor. Of course, I had to put them back properly, which only made more work for me, something I did not need more of, as I am sure you can understand.

I had to find chores that Brandon would be successful at, because Matthew was right—it was unfair for his brother not to participate in the household chores. From that day forward, I matched chores with Brandon's limited capabilities. Because he lacked fine and gross motor skills, he did not learn how to tie his shoes until he was fifteen years old. That should give you a picture of how difficult it was for him to do even "simple" tasks successfully.

The first chore I gave him was to sweep up the leaves in our yard and throw them away in the trashcans. I felt he had a good chance of succeeding at this, and he did. That was how I began including Brandon in the household chores. He also helped wash the cars and bathe the dog. It seemed wiser to assign him outdoor chores at first because any necessary clean-up would be much easier for me to deal with. Over time, I found jobs for him to do indoors as well. Soon he was able to sort the laundry and empty the dishes and silverware from the dishwasher. Brandon began to feel good about himself and what he was able to accomplish. He no longer complained about having to do chores.

Yes, it would have been much easier for me to let him slide and for me to do everything for him. However, if I had done this he would not have learned and developed in areas that helped him to become more independent today.

The Best Way to Learn About Life Is to Live It

The best way to learn life is to live it—and yet, when it comes to our special needs child, this prospect scares most parents. Fear and resistance not only stops us, but also our child, from advancing to the next stage.

Allowing our child to grow and one day go off on his or her own is the ideal scenario, but how can we achieve this when we have an adult child with special needs?

My husband passed away at an early age, so I was a single parent when it came time to launch Brandon into adulthood and help him fulfill his dream of living on his own. Most of my immediate family thought I was crazy to let him live by himself. Brandon had never asked for much, so when he told me he wanted to live alone, I was blindsided. As a matter of fact, he tossed this bombshell the day of his dad's funeral while we were out having dinner. I watched him stab his food with a fork and I thought to myself, he can barely eat and is extremely naïve, so how can he survive by himself out in the "real world"? I had to dig deep, very deep, within myself and I was shocked when I found myself saying yes. *I knew in my heart that I had to give him this opportunity even though I was scared stiff.*

The first few months were extremely trying, and I was a nervous wreck. One morning, after Brandon had been living in his own apartment for just a few months, I called to see how he was doing. He said to me, "Mom, there are weird people on the streets at three o'clock in the morning." OMG! I wanted to scream and demand to know what in the world he was doing out at that time! I am not sure how I did it, but I managed to hold my tongue and not react overtly, which would have stopped him from confiding in me in the future. I kept silent but inside I was dying, though relieved that nothing harmful happened. Brandon then said, "Mom, I will never do that again." I replied, as calmly as I could, "Yes, three o'clock in the morning is not a safe time to be out." I never found out what he was doing outside at that time but I knew this is how my son would learn—by firsthand experience. And learn he did. Brandon has never gone out in the middle of the night again.

No Risk, No Gain

Fear and more fear can hold us back from making choices outside of our comfort zone. "No risk, no gain," said Anna Hundley, a woman who has worked with autistic adults for more than thirty years, and she is right. We must focus on what our children can do, and support and encourage them as they struggle through their challenges. If I did not address my fears and blocks I would have never had the courage to allow my son to live independently. The first year was not easy; it was extremely difficult for both of us. But as the years passed, it became easier and we continued to learn along the way. I was encouraged as I watched Brandon grow through every negative and positive experience.

Choose Your Battles Wisely

It used to drive me crazy that Brandon made his bed with huge lumps in it. He owned an alarm clock and refused to set it when he had an appointment. He also kept empty soda and juice cans in his refrigerator which bothered me. Then I realized it was not my business, that these "eccentricities" weren't detrimental to Brandon in any way, and I needed to choose my battles wisely. I stopped trying to correct him constantly or tell him what to do and how to do it. Except when it came to his well-being, health and safety, I seldom offered any explicit suggestions or advice. However, there were times when I found myself reverting back to my old patterns and preaching at him, but I quickly corrected myself and apologized. It wasn't long before I began to understand the concept of "good enough."

Let Good Enough Be Good Enough

While talking with Brandon on the phone a few years ago, I remember suggesting to him how he could do a few things "better." I remember him saying, "I am going to wait until tomorrow and do all my chores in one day although I have a free day today. I am going to wait until I need to do it." To which I replied, "Don't you think it would be easier to do it now, or at least some of it today when you are feeling well and have the time?" Brandon often procrastinates and his plans are frequently interrupted because he doesn't feel well, which was why I made the suggestion. Then I began to realize that maybe this is *not* procrastination at all, *it is simply the way his mind works.*

After I hung up, I stopped short. What I was thinking? That what he was doing had to be good enough for *me?* This hit me right between the eyes. I quickly called him back and apologized and told him that if what he was doing worked for him, it was good enough for me. Making this change has greatly improved our relationship. I sincerely appreciate all he does and I know he can feel it. It was important that I step back and allow him to mature and develop on his own, in his own way and time.

Now that my son is forty-one years old, my job is to be there for him when he comes to me for help. Other than that, he is on his own. If I want him to continue to progress after I'm gone, I need to implement this frame of mind now, while I am alive. Of course, if he is ill or there is an emergency, I will always step in.

Ask Your Special Needs Child for Help

If you ask your adult child for help you may be surprised with the outcome. I went to pick up Brandon to do some errands. On that particular day I felt as if I was coming down with the flu. I was exhausted and nauseated. I knew he needed my help so I did not cancel our plans. When I arrived I told him I did not feel well and I asked if he could help me. He said he would.

I took Brandon to the market and he pushed the cart and did the actual shopping by finding the groceries and putting all the purchases into the basket. Afterwards he emptied the cart and lined up all the bags of food in the trunk of my car. I told him how much I appreciated his help and I could tell he felt good about doing it for me.

Since that day even if I feel well I ask for his help. Appealing to him in this way caused a dramatic shift in our relationship. It has made him feel important and capable of doing something for someone else. By teaching him that life is a give-and-take, two-way street, he has become more responsible and aware of the existence of others.

I've asked Brandon to help me balance my checkbook ever since I discovered he has a knack for it. He is extremely frugal and loves getting deals. He is a skilled bargain hunter and knows how to stretch a dollar. His brother Matt kids Brandon by telling him he has cobwebs in his wallet since he doesn't open it often and he prefers it when others pay. Making gentle, respectful "fun" of this trait makes him feel good about himself and proud of his skill with money. He always laughs when he's told he has "cobwebs in his wallet."

My son cannot tell whether someone is making fun of him or is just joking around. That is why it is crucial when we are joking around that he knows without a doubt that we are just being silly and not making fun of him. He has been teased enough all his life. As a family, we certainly don't want to add to it. It is a joy to hear Brandon laugh, although it does not happen very often.

You can only take your child as far as *you* are willing to go. You also must continue to grow if that is what you are expecting of your child.

Many of us only change when we are forced to, but over time many of us learn that life is easier when we are willing to change because we want to, not because we have to.

Later on, in Section Four on Independence, I will talk about the importance of independence training for parents. I will describe in detail what you can do now to help your child achieve maximum independence and answer one of the most frequently asked questions: "How do I let go?"

Three

The Natural Progression of Life

*There really are places in the heart you
don't even know exist until you love a child.*

Anne Lamott

For years I have been speaking to audiences filled with special needs parents. It never seemed to matter what state or country I was in, the statements and cries from parents echoed one another around the world. It may have been said in different languages but their heartfelt cries have been similar and consistent over many years: ***perhaps you may feel they are quoting you.***

- "I am terrified of what the future might hold for my daughter. I worry about it all the time."

- "I want my son to have a meaningful life, not just sit and watch television. I want him to have a job and a social life."

- "Two worries for my adult son are: Will he be safe and will he be happy? That is the bottom line for me."

- "If you have a child with autism and special needs you feel as if you can never die. You have to live forever. I have no intention of dying until I know my son is safe and secure somewhere."

- "My son cannot speak for himself, so I have been his voice. What will he do without me?"

- "You are hearing about more and more people finding themselves, because of the lack of options and choices, in places they don't belong."

- "Who will care for my son when the day comes that I can no longer help him safely cross the street? Safety is my number one issue for my son."

- "When our children grow up will there be public support for them as adults, when they are no longer cute, harmless, and unthreatening?"

- "Something I worry about is people misunderstanding my son because he looks normal. And he acts pretty normal most of the time. So I always worry."

- "My daughter cannot communicate well enough with people to explain herself or tell them what to do or what she needs or wants."

- "So many of us parents are lost, alone and unsupported. All I want is to know that when I am not here that my son is okay and taken care of, but I cry every day wondering what will happen to him."

Hearing these statements from so many people confirms that you are not alone. But the undeniable truth is that it is the natural progression of life that children will likely outlive their parents. Quite frankly, we would not want it any other way—unless we have a child with a disability, which changes everything. You begin to think, "I have a child with autism, epilepsy and special needs. *I can never die.* Who will take care of my child? What will my child do without me?"

Last year I attended three funerals within two months, making it impossible to ignore the inevitable, that death is part of life. No one lives forever. This has been a hard subject for me to tackle but since I have seen several of my healthy friends die lately from odd accidents and incidents, I knew that I had to be prepared. That was always my motto while raising Brandon and now the time has come to practice what I teach.

The Natural Progression of Life

Consider this: Your children will spend 75% of their lives as adults—and most of that time will be without you. You need to have a plan and be prepared. It is time to take action.

I recently became a senior citizen, and a new reality set in when I noticed new strands of gray hair begin to sprout from my scalp. I wrote these chapters with an urgency that I believe this subject truly deserves. It forced me to accept that I am aging and to stare my own passing in the face.

The subject is never an easy one to talk about. No one likes to contemplate his or her own mortality, but it's time to face the fact that we cannot *not* think about it if we have a special needs child. I would never want to leave this planet without some type of instructional care manual for the people whom I will choose to help my son.

The care manual in this book will give you permission to begin truly planning for the future even though, like me, you probably hope to remain on the planet for many more years to come.

In a perfect world, we would all have a special person to look after our special needs adult children in the same way we've taken care of them ourselves. But unfortunately this is seldom the case. If your child has "godparents," it is likely they would not be willing or even able to assume this responsibility when the time came. Even if you are fortunate enough to have siblings or family members who *are* willing to step in after you're gone, you will need to convey to them what is involved. We can try to show and tell people what we want from them, but nowadays people are busier than ever with their own lives. Everything needs to be written down in detail to make it easier for your child's guardians and helpers to access and understand this critical information.

I have been on the special needs path for more than forty years. What I know for sure is that the more you are prepared, the better. I love my son and I know it is my responsibility to get all his ducks in a row and to tie up all the loose ends I possibly can now. I know I must make sure to address all of them, leaving no stone unturned.

When you raise a special needs child, you and only you know your son or daughter's specific wants and needs, and that the smallest things can often be the most important. You also know what type of scheduling and routines are necessary. My son, Brandon, has many needs that no one knows about except me. Similarly, a mother learns to understand what her children are saying even if they do not speak. Brandon speaks, but he often does not say what he means or means what he says. The connection between parents—especially moms—and their special needs child is a very strong bond. We are often the only people who can understand them.

How do we get our child taken care of in the way we would want if our child outlives us?

The answer is that every parent must have a detailed written plan. All of your child's information needs to be written down in one place so it can be used as an instruction manual for those who will be responsible for your child's care. Remember, if people do not know what your child needs and wants, they will never be able to provide it. Leave your desires and wishes written down so your adult child can live a familiar lifestyle with dignity, respect, love, understanding and acceptance.

The next chapter will explain how to begin creating such a written plan.

SECTION TWO

Take Action

*How to Create Your Personalized Instructional
Care Manual & Step-In Parenting Network*

Four

How to Create Your Personalized Instructional Care Manual

*We all die. The goal isn't to live forever;
the goal is to create something that will.*

Chuck Palahniuk

What is an Instructional Care Manual?

Your Instructional Care Manual (ICM) is a written plan that will serve as your "voice" and communicate your child's needs and your wishes to your son's or daughter's future networkers. You will have a safe place to write down pertinent information that only you know about your child. You will be passing the manual on to people in your Step-In Parenting Network, (SIPN) who will help your child live well after you are gone. In the next chapter I will talk about how to set up your Step-In Parenting Network and explain in detail what a networker is and where and how to find them.

I have provided a friendly and easy-to-use Sample Care Manual to help you get started. Write down anything and everything that you feel will inform others on how to help your child not only survive, but thrive. *Celebrate the fact that you are taking action and doing all you can, while you can.*

I was pleasantly surprised by the tremendous relief I felt after filling out the manual, and I believe you will feel the same way, too.

Answer the questions honestly and clearly. It is important to be as thorough and as heartfelt as you possibly can. In addition to all the "facts," you will want to convey the tenderness, kindness and respect you have for your child to those who will be reading and using the manual, in the hope that they will feel it and continue on in the same vein.

Easy, NO! But a necessity, YES! I promise as you move along you will feel more at ease about your child's future, knowing this information you leave behind will follow your child for the rest of his or her life.

How to Create Your Personalized Instructional Care Manual

Writing down important information about your child in this Instructional Care Manual (ICM) section is one of the very best ways to ensure that your Step-In Parenting networkers will be able to meet your child's needs. The clearer and more detailed the better. You will want to include even small items that may seem insignificant when compared to your bigger priorities. It's the "little things" that could very well have the biggest impact on your child's life.

Start by taking a few minutes to read through this chapter and look through my Sample Care Manual. When you are ready, begin working on the "first draft" of your child's care manual. You will find it towards the back of this book. Write as though you are meeting a networker for the very first time.

At first, I would suggest that you do not overthink this step, but allow the information to flow freely from you. Write to your heart's content. Remember, preparing this manual is an act of love, not an act of sadness or despair. It is a golden opportunity for you to express yourself and your child's needs and wants. It is an essential part of doing all that you can to ensure a good future for your child.

To be the most effective, I suggest you write when you feel calm and focused. If you find yourself becoming agitated or overwhelmed, or your mind is elsewhere, don't worry, just wait until you feel more centered. At the right time you will be able to fill out the manual at your own pace. You can work on it bit by bit and begin on any page. I have included extra pages so you will have space to add new categories, update the information, or change it at any time.

As you know, for most of our children, adjusting to anything new can be extremely difficult.

That is why it is so very important for you to write down clearly what you want your networkers to know about your child. Background information is essential. Having this crucial information in hand will help your networkers bring your wishes to life. One of the goals of this manual is for them to feel as though they have met your child in person before they actually do.

I will happily take your hand and show you the way, step-by-step. I will share with you the wishes I wrote down in the sample manual for my son. We will all feel differently about what is most important to us and our child and that is what makes this exercise so unique. There are no right or wrong answers. As long as you follow your heart and approach this exercise as an opportunity to have your voice heard, you'll do just fine.

Your manual will supply your networkers with information they would otherwise never know.

I wrote the following short stories as examples of how crucial the small things can be, and how to make a point clearly and concisely when you are painting a picture of your child with your words. The clearer you are, the better.

Example 1. When my boys were young my sister offered to take care of my sons, Matthew and Brandon, so my husband and I could go away for the weekend. Matthew was seven and Brandon was five. When I returned home, my sister was beside herself. She had just made hot dogs for the kids for dinner and when she gave Brandon his hot dog, all cut up in pieces, he fell to the floor screaming and crying. She did not understand what was going on until Matthew told her he likes to eat his hot dog all in one piece. My sister said she was baffled and upset by his reaction, and if it weren't for Matthew she would not have known what to do to remedy the situation. She quickly made him another hot dog and all was well.

Example 2. You will always see Brandon sporting a baseball cap with his favorite team's name embroidered across the front. He has been wearing baseball caps since he was a little boy. It wasn't until he was thirty-nine years old that I uncovered the reason why he wears them. I never gave it much thought and assumed that he wore hats just because he liked them.

Recently, Brandon and I were having dinner at his brother Matthew's house.

When he sat down at the table Matt told him to remove his hat, as is proper etiquette. Brandon is comfortable and sociable around his brother, but after taking off his hat his demeanor changed immediately and dramatically. The entire time he was at the table he looked down at his plate and never once looked up. He did not say a word and appeared a combination of sad, irritated and troubled.

There were eight of us at the dinner table and no one other than I noticed or acknowledged Brandon's change in behavior. It was an animated group, and I knew it would embarrass Brandon terribly if I were to ask him what was going on, so I waited until we got in the car.

On our way home, I asked him how his evening was. He said, "I didn't have a good time. It wasn't fun." I asked him why, and after a few minutes of silence, he said, "I did not want to take off my hat at the dinner table. I need my hat." When I asked him why he needed to keep his hat on, he said nothing. Several more minutes passed. I thought about what possibly could have been the problem and ventured to ask, "Does it have something to do with the lights?"

"Yes, Mom. The lights hurt my eyes and I got a headache," he replied.

After dropping him off I called Matt immediately and told him what his brother had said. He was completely unaware of Brandon's sensitivity to light and thanked me for explaining his behavior at the table. Problem resolved! Neither Matt nor I will ever ask Brandon to remove his hat again.

These are tidbits of "intimate" information that only a parent is likely to know. That is why your child's care manual is so very important. Any information of this nature that you can share with your networkers will help make their job much easier, and your child's life much better.

Suggestions for Conveying Information to Your Networkers

1. Write what you are trying to convey in a few short paragraphs.
2. Write it in a list.
3. Be honest and crystal clear.
4. Get a family member or a friend to read it and see if they understand what you have written. Make sure you choose people who will take the time to read the information carefully and be honest with you.
5. Write simply and be concise.
6. If you feel like adding something humorous then do so, as long as you feel it is appropriate.
7. At the end of your final care manual write a Summary/Overview List. I will talk more about how to do that later on in this chapter.

8. Repeating yourself is fine if you are trying to convey something of great importance.

Being a networker is not an easy job, so whatever you can do to make it easier for your networkers to understand your child, do it. Always keep that in mind when writing. You can write whatever you wish in the working manual. When you are ready to update and finalize the information, you can then be more selective regarding what you leave in, add or delete for the final manual.

Filling out the manual is a process just like everything else. But first, ask yourself what is the *one most important piece of information* I want my networkers to know about my child?

Here is my own example, briefly stated, which I will explain in detail in the Sample ICM form:

Brandon has intractable epilepsy and he has seizures. If he has a seizure while he is with you, you will need to know how to assist him.

It is crucial that networkers know what to do if and when Brandon has a seizure when they are together. The more they know the less fearful they will become. Because his seizures are unpredictable and could happen anywhere at any time, they must be able to think quickly on their feet and do the best they can to protect him. After their first experience, most helpers are relieved since they now know what to expect and how to best help Brandon if another seizure occurs on their watch. (The procedure is explained in the First Aid for Epilepsy later in the chapter).

Accepting My Son for Who He Is

I have two older sisters. My middle sister asked if she could take Brandon to Hawaii when he was ten. I initially thought she was kidding. Except for my mother, no one had ever asked to take Brandon anywhere. My sister was a teacher at the time and also had a degree in marriage and family counseling. One of her girlfriends was going on the trip, so she felt the two of them could manage quite well.

She told me she had big plans for Brandon—they would take him swimming and snorkeling, play with him on the beach, and do all the fun-in-the-sun activities they could fit in. Her intentions were admirable, but *she didn't understand who Brandon truly was.* I kept trying to tell her that Brandon was unable to do *any* of those activities, and even if he were able, he would have no interest whatsoever in doing them. She did not take me seriously and spirited Brandon away to Hawaii for a week, thinking she could give him a wonderful vacation and they all would have a good time. I am sorry to say that did not happen.

It started to go downhill from the moment Brandon stepped on the plane. He had trouble negotiating the narrow aisle and he bumped into everyone with his body and suitcase. He never apologized because he thought this was their fault, not his. Brandon has great difficulty determining where his body ends and does not understand that he can be the one responsible for jostling or bumping into another person. My sister walked behind him apologizing to everyone, but to no avail. He made many enemies even before the plane took off. She later told me just getting him seated and belted in was a huge, exhausting ordeal. Once they landed, she was quite surprised when he could hardly carry his own suitcase, complaining it was too heavy. She was shocked when he was unable to use the key to open their hotel room door. All this took place within the first ten hours and set the tone for the rest of the trip.

The next day, when she discovered he hated the beach and the swimming pool, she began to get a much clearer picture of what lay ahead of them. She began to ask herself, "What did I get myself into?" It was then that she began to understand what I was trying to convey to her about Brandon before she finalized her well-meaning, but unrealistic vacation plans.

Yes, my sister finally saw Brandon's numerous limitations, but unfortunately, it was too late, and the trip was a disaster.

I cannot emphasize enough how important it is to be as thorough and straightforward as you can in your Instructional Care Manual. If repeatedly talking to my own sister was not enough to convey to her the realities of Brandon's day-to-day struggles and challenges, *how would I ever expect total strangers to understand him and care for him properly without giving them a permanent, written reference?*

Over the years I have heard many frustrated parents lament that their immediate family members, like mine, could not understand their special needs child, no matter how often they tried to educate them. A client of mine asked to read this book prior to publication, which she then gave to her mother, who had great difficulty understanding her teenage grandson who has autism. "I think I understand him better now," she said. "My grandson has almost all the same problems as the man in the book."

What I have learned from this is that it can be an enormous help to see this information about our children written down in black and white. It can also be used as a great tool for anyone who currently interacts with them—teachers, therapists, physicians, etc.

The Instructional Care Manual (ICM)

I check over and update my manual monthly, sometimes more frequently, as there always seems to be something new to add. So that it doesn't slip my mind, I make a date on my calendar each month to remind myself to review it. I have found it is best to keep all the information together and in one place. However, when I do not have my book handy when I need to add something, I put the information on an electronic device for safekeeping until I can transfer the item(s) to the manual.

Notes

Notes

Sample
Instructional Care Manual

This Instructional Care Manual is the perfect place for you to leave all the personal and crucial information about your special needs child for those who will step in for you after you are gone.

Your Child's Full Name _____

Nickname _____

Birthdate _____

Parent's Signature _____

Date _____

Contents

Sample Instructional Care Manual

Section 1. Personal: Important Information About My Child
1. Letter of Intent
2. My Child's Diagnosis
3. Brief Description of My Child in a Paragraph (300 words or less) and in a List
4. Photo Page
5. The Most Important Thing You Must Know About My Child
6. My Child's "Gray" Areas, Which Would Not Be Apparent Unless I Told You
7. A List of Tidbits
8. Schedules and Routines
9. What My Child Must Have
10. What Works Well for My Child
11. Likes and Dislikes
12. What My Child Cannot Have
13. What Makes My Child Angry, Sad, Frustrated, or Upset
14. What Scares My Child
15. What Not to Do and Where My Child Cannot Go
16. Write Helpful Teaching Stories and Q&A
17. Sample Summary and Overview List

In addition, your Working Instructional Care Manual will also include Favorite Things and What Soothes and Gives My Child Pleasure.

Section 2. Additional Pertinent Information:

- **Emergency Contact Information and Medical Care:** Physicians, Dentists, Therapists, Pharmacies, Medications, Health Conditions, Allergies, and First Aid Procedures

- **Special Dietary Needs, Meals and Food:** Dietary Restrictions and Favorite Foods

- **Legal Matters:** Attorneys, Financial Advisors, Insurance Information, etc.

- **Family Background:** Past and Present

- **School and Education:** Past, Present, and Future

- **Employment:** Past, Present, and Future

- **Residential:** Past, Present, and Future

- **Social Activities/Recreation:** Likes and Dislikes

- **Religious Affiliation:** Past, Present, and Future

- **Making Final Arrangements:** Be Prepared

- **Summary and Overview List**

Sample Instructional Care Manual (ICM)

I have filled out the Sample Manual to help lead the way and provide you with ideas for filling out your own manual. You will be able to download your Final Instructional Care Manual from my website at www.AmaliaStarr.com. Placing the information on a computer will make it easy to update the document and keep it current. Whether you choose to complete the manual in longhand or on the computer, be sure to sign it and date it each time you revise it. Place it with your other important papers and let someone you trust know of its existence and location.

I Suggest You Begin by Writing a Letter of Intent

I will place my letter of intent on the cover page along with the words "Final Instructional Manual" so at a quick glance anyone will know what this care manual is all about. Let me explain what this letter is and its purpose.

A Letter of Intent is a document you prepare to help the guardians, trustees, networkers, and the courts interpret your hopes and desires for your child. It is not a formal "legal" document, but the courts will look to it for guidance in understanding your child and your wishes. The courts tend to favor the family's wishes as long as they are not illegal or immoral, so you can see how important this document is going to be. *It will follow your child for the rest of his/her life.*

Your letter can be addressed to "TO WHOM IT MAY CONCERN," or you may want to make it more personal by addressing it to someone specific, or directly to your child.

A Letter of Intent is a living document that needs to be updated routinely. When you leave your Letter of Intent in your final ICM, you can personalize it any way you wish.

Here is my letter as an example:

To Whom It May Concern,

This is my Final Instructional Care Manual with all the pertinent information about my son, Brandon, that only I would know. I trust and believe that having this information together in one place will give you easy access to what you need to know about my son in the least amount of time. I am aware that Brandon can be quite difficult to understand and by writing out these details, facts and instructions my hope is to alleviate that potential problem.

Truly, words cannot express the gratitude I feel in my heart and the peace of mind I experience knowing that you are willing to step in and help my son continue to live the lifestyle to which he is accustomed. It is a tremendous relief and truly one of the greatest gifts you can give a mother and her special needs child.

With sincere appreciation, gratitude, and love,

Amalia Starr
Signature: _____

Date: _____

As you can see, I chose not to address my letter to a specific person. Instead, I made it more general because I really do not know who will be standing in for me at that time or when it will be. My plan is to have several people help my son and when needed to advocate for him. Having networkers is a fluid, ever-changing process which I will talk more about in Chapter Five.

Your Child's Diagnosis

This is the perfect place to begin. Although you may refer to it throughout your manual, it is vital for your networkers to know your child's diagnosis. As I mentioned earlier, you will find that some information will overlap or need to be repeated when you are writing about related issues. It will help to emphasize and reinforce the points you wish to make. You can be brief and simply write a line or two, as I have below, or you can make it as detailed as you wish. It is entirely up to you.

My son, Brandon, has autism, intractable epilepsy and severe learning disorders.

I believe that placing a diagnosis on the first page of the manual will help your networkers understand your child from the beginning; this way they won't have to search through the manual for this critical information.

A Brief Description of Your Child

Paint a picture of your child in 300 words or less.

Note: Words in highlighted brackets [ ] indicate time-sensitive information that is to be updated as needed.

Brandon has a rather large build and is **[forty-one]** years of age. He is approximately six-feet, two-inches tall, and much of the time gives the impression that he can handle the world. Unfortunately, this is not often the case. Sometimes he looks like a lost puppy and is easily irritated and agitated. His tone of voice can be off-putting, even if he is having a good time. He does not often display good manners even though he has been taught them repeatedly. He sometimes walks hunched over and often wears odd clothing combinations. You will most often find him in a baseball cap and shorts even in cold weather.

On rare occasions Brandon will laugh when others laugh at something humorous he has said, even if he was not intentionally being funny. Because he enjoys this response and attention, he will continue to repeat what he said over and over until those around him get annoyed and say something rude or turn and walk away.

If I were to describe my son's demeanor I would have to say that most of the time he has a "blank" look, or appears irritated. His facial expressions seldom match how he feels. *He has told me that he is happy all the time, which, given his low affect, can be hard for others to believe or understand.*

I found it helpful to include information in paragraph form as well as in lists. I discovered that some of my networkers found it easier to comprehend information from the lists. Some of the information therefore will overlap.

A List Describing My Child
1. He is **[forty-one]** years of age.
2. He has autism.
3. He has intractable epilepsy.
4. He has severe learning disorders.
5. He often does not say what he means or means what he says.
6. He lives in his own apartment and has for the past **[seventeen]** years.
7. He likes to be treated kindly and spoken to softly.
8. He must learn to trust you before he can open up.
9. He functions best with a routine.
10. If you make a plan with him it's important to keep it.
11. Any kind of change is extremely difficult for him.
12. He loves his independence and wants to be treated as an equal.

13. He thrives on positive input.
14. He likes to be accepted for who he is.
15. He does not want people to try to change him.

Photo Page

I feel it is extremely valuable to have family pictures in your manual. They say a picture is worth a thousand words and I couldn't agree more. Include any photos you feel will give your networkers some insight into who your child is and what your family life has been like. Make this page count by telling a story with your treasured and precious photographs.

While looking through some photos of Brandon I decided to call and ask him if it would be okay if I included a few in this section of the book. He was quiet for several moments and then said, "No, I don't want you to."

I am respecting my son's wishes and therefore will not feature photos of him here. However, there will be photographs of him in my personal ICM.

Brandon does not like to be photographed and never has. Just recently I found his baby photo album and gave it to him. He looked it over for a split second and then handed it right back to me. "I don't want it," he said. I was rather surprised and asked him why, but he was unable to answer. I took the album home with me. End of story, no more questions asked. *We all have a right to feel the way we do, even if we can't explain it to someone else. Just another lesson I learned from Brandon.*

THE MOST IMPORTANT THING YOU NEED TO KNOW
My Son Has Epilepsy

If Brandon has a seizure while he is with you, you will need to know how to assist him. In addition to the specific information I have provided below, please follow the Epilepsy Foundation's first aid guidelines for seizures, which I have also included in this chapter.

When Brandon experiences sudden jerking motions, it is likely he is about to have a seizure. Have him sit down immediately, preferably on something comfortable, or on the floor or ground. He needs to be as close to the ground as possible so that if he is having a seizure he will not have far to fall.

If he has not eaten for several hours, the seizure may be due to low blood sugar. Please carry a granola bar or small bag of trail mix whenever you are with him. He usually has one in his pocket, but it may be hard for him to get to it under the circumstances, so at the first sign of symptoms, open and give him yours. A tonic-clonic seizure may be averted if he is able to eat some nuts or a granola bar right away.

Seizures may last several minutes or more. It is not necessary to call the paramedics unless my son is injured, but call them if you are uncomfortable or perceive a need for medical help. When Brandon regains consciousness allow him some time to get his bearings, then help him up and take him home. He will be exhausted and hungry, so give him something to eat that he can easily hold in his hands, such as a sandwich. I recommend just preparing something nourishing with what's on hand, rather then asking him what he would like to eat, as he may not have the wherewithal to make a decision while he is recovering.

FIRST AID FOR EPILEPSY
Adapted Courtesy of the Epilepsy Foundation

The goal is to keep the person safe until the seizure stops naturally by itself. It is important to know how to respond to all seizures, including the most noticeable kind—generalized tonic-clonic (formerly known as "grand mal") seizures, or convulsions.

When providing seizure first aid for generalized tonic-clonic seizures, these are the key things to remember:

- Keep calm and reassure other people who may be nearby.
- Don't hold the person down or try to stop his movements.
- Time the seizure with your watch.
- Clear the area around the person of anything hard or sharp.
- Loosen ties or anything around the neck that may make breathing difficult.
- Put something flat and soft, like a folded jacket, under the head.
- Turn the person gently onto one side. This will help keep the airway clear. Do not try to force the mouth open with any hard implement or with fingers. It is not true that a person having a

seizure can swallow his tongue. Efforts to hold the tongue down can cause injury.
- Don't attempt artificial respiration except in the unlikely event that a person does not start breathing again after the seizure has stopped.
- Stay with the person until the seizure ends naturally.
- Be friendly and reassuring as consciousness returns.
- Offer to call a taxi, friend or relative to help the person get home if he seems confused or unable to get home by himself.

Brandon Never Knows When a Seizure is Coming On

Brandon has had seizures since he was nine years old and they continue to be one if his biggest challenges. It is not known what causes them, but it could be related to low blood sugar due to not eating, anxiety, stress or any combination of these. No medication has ever been able to stop his seizures.

It has been found that seizure medication can rob the body of nutrients, so taking vitamins and other supplements and eating a more balanced diet is part of Brandon's daily routine. It seems to be working, as he has been known to go more than two months without a seizure. (For more information about the use of vitamins and supplements in seizure prevention, see *Gina De Masi* in the Appendix).

The "Gray" Areas—What You Would Not Know About My Son If I Did Not Tell You

The gray areas will be extremely helpful for networkers to know. These are the things that neurotypical people would likely never pick up on or be able to figure out on their own about your child. That is why it is critical to write about them all.

In the next several pages I have described Brandon's seven gray areas in great detail to get you thinking about what your own child's gray areas are, and how you might go about describing them. If there is anything I can do to help my networkers understand my son better, this is the time and place for me to do it.

Your child's gray areas may be quite different from my son's. However, when you are filling in this section please keep in mind how difficult it would be for others to understand your child without this information. They need to know these vital details.

1. Lack of Communication and Socialization Skills

We all use words verbally to get us what we want and need, to converse with a friend and to speak to people we encounter every day. We do this face to face, over the phone, or through the Internet. We use the written word to write letters, agreements, text messages, emails, books, etc. It is the way we communicate. Our tone and pitch will change depending on what we are trying to convey. We could be soft spoken and loving, loud and angry, or anything in between.

There are many autistic and special needs children who cannot access or retrieve appropriate words readily (and some not at all), nor are they able to adopt an appropriate, acceptable tone of voice to match their words. What they would like to say often does not come out of their mouths in an appropriate way, and so they are judged as offensive or weird. We know that they may just need extra time to respond and that it takes sensitivity and patience on the listener's part to "interpret" what our child is really trying to say. This is something most people do not take the time to understand. It is important that Brandon's networkers grasp his individual communication style so that they will not repeatedly misunderstand him or take offense. *Getting to know one another will take time.*

After working in the autism and special needs community for many years and raising an autistic son, I finally got the picture. Simply said, my son knows what he wants to say but often he is unable to *say* it the way he *means* it.

Because Brandon's words often come out of his mouth jumbled up people assume he is either stupid or clueless, and he is neither of those. He is actually smart and quite discerning. *There are times he comes up with the most amazing and wisest comments that take me completely by surprise. Perhaps you, too, have experienced this with your child?*

At this writing, Brandon is forty-one years old. Over time I have seen a vast improvement in his language skills. However, he is often slow to reply and most people find it irritating waiting to hear what he has to say. My son is not able to defend himself using words, which continues to be a major problem. If someone accuses him of doing something he did not do he is unable to reply in a timely manner. If and when he can reply it is usually too late. Sometimes he will agree with the accuser, hoping they will leave him alone, without considering what the consequences of that may be.

2. He Can Be Difficult to Understand

Brandon is seldom angry, and although his tone of voice may give that impression, in most cases he is not. It is easy to assume that his inflections indicate that he is sad, angry, upset, or feeling another negative emotion. If you want to be sure you are "reading" him accurately, don't hesitate to ask him a direct question, such as, "Are you mad?" He will likely answer you by saying, "No, why?"

Brandon told me the other day that he is always happy. However, if I judged his happiness by the tone of his voice or the expression on his face, I would be wrong every time.

If you think I don't know how difficult it is to understand Brandon, I truly do know. I appreciate from the deepest part of my soul that I have networkers who are willing to help my son after I am gone. I know it will not be easy, especially in the beginning, but I also know that in time and with patience, it will get easier.

Brandon is sweet and gentle, and an all-around good guy. Though he is often misunderstood by his words and actions, it does not change what a fundamentally good person he is.

Once you understand Brandon and allow him to be himself he will change your world for the better. You will never see the world quite the same. I admire, respect, and love my son dearly. He is one of the most interesting and courageous people I have ever known.

He lives in the present. What happened to him yesterday is old news and is usually not discussed. He is able to start each day fresh and new. What an amazing quality to have. I am working on adding that to my life. This is just another lesson Brandon has taught me. He is a great teacher and has helped me grow and change for the better.

3. He Will Not Directly Ask for Help

This is a very important area for networkers to know. Brandon will not usually ask for help, but when he does, it may feel as if he is just making a comment. Since he will not reach out to people when he needs help, it is important to teach others how and when to reach out to him.

Years ago Brandon told his counselor that "girls cost a lot of money." It seemed as though he was just making an observation but he was indirectly asking his counselor for help. Although the counselor had been working with Brandon for six years, he unfortunately missed this cue and simply agreed with him. That led to Brandon spending $750.00 on a girl who pretended to be his girlfriend but who was only using him for his money.

These are the kind of things that can be avoided when you understand how to listen to Brandon's cues for help, which are rarely posed as questions. It is essential to listen carefully when he makes a comment or what seems like a simple statement about a personal experience—he may be asking for help.

If he had said to me that "girls cost a lot of money," I would have asked him, "What do you mean?" By putting the ball back in his court, he would have tried to explain what he meant as best he could, and I would have understood that he had a problem and needed help.

Up to now, I am the only person he will call and openly ask for help, so it is critical that his future networkers understand his way of communicating when he needs a helping hand.

4. He Can Rarely Say What He Means and Rarely Uses an Appropriate Tone of Voice

Brandon cannot express his intention with a tone of voice that accurately conveys what he means. This has created enormous problems for him throughout his life. He knows what he means to say, but he cannot retrieve the right words or have the words he says come out the way he wants them to, though he *thinks* they do. Sound confusing? It is. This used to be a huge sore spot between Brandon and his older brother, Matt.

Whenever he and Matt would have a conflict, Brandon would tell me one thing and his brother would tell me another. I often sided with Brandon until I discovered that he had a tendency to describe what seemed to be a *completely* different incident to each one of us. Because Brandon cannot keep "the facts" straight in his mind, he has often been called a liar and accused of being deliberately deceptive, but that is never his intent.

Brandon is not a liar. He actually is honest and truthful, almost to a fault. He just has great difficulty retrieving information accurately and selecting the precise words or tone of voice that would properly convey his thoughts and feelings to others. This is extremely important to know for those who will be helping him in the future.

Brandon communicates better with his brother these days, so rather than have me act as a referee, we are experimenting with a new approach. I told my sons that when they have a problem, they need to do their best to work it out between themselves. We are just trying this out, and so far so good.

Brandon's own tone of voice is often off-putting to others, including myself. We work hard raising our children, and being able to see some type of appreciation from them would help us tremendously. Sadly, while growing up he was never able to say "thank you" or "you're welcome" at the appropriate times. I used to take this personally because people would comment on how rude my son was. I was often asked, "Why don't you teach your son better manners?" It was mortifying. We know that our special needs children are doing the best they can, but people with neurotypical children or no children often do not understand this.

Over the years many of Brandon's helpers were offended by the tone of his voice and his lack of manners. I want to nip future misunderstandings in the bud now regarding this issue so his networkers will understand not to take his apparent rudeness or lack of manners personally. I believe just having this information will spare Brandon many problems and may even prevent networkers from quitting.

5. A Soft Voice and Compliments Go a Long Way

Brandon may complain that you are mad or yelling at him when that clearly is not your intention. I have discovered that he is highly sensitive to other people's tones of voice, despite being unaware of his own easily-misunderstood inflections. You must be aware of your tone when speaking with my son. A soft, gentle, kind voice will help him feel at ease and more willing to open up.

Recently Brandon's new Service Coordinator, Jennifer, from the Regional Center (see Appendix), came to visit him for his quarterly meeting. After she left his house he called me. He said, "I really like Jennifer. She is very nice and has a soft voice. She told me how proud she was of me and how well I am doing." My son loves to be complimented, just as we all do. Praise and positive input work like a magic tonic.

6. The Downside of Humor

If someone laughs at something Brandon says he will repeat it over and over until the person gets irritated and either hollers at him to stop, makes fun of him, or walks away in disgust. Many people have no time for people like Brandon, and over the years he has been mistreated and called rude names. Some people believe that because he does not speak correctly and cannot say what he means that he has no feelings. How they put that connection together I'll never know. It is absurd and could not be further from the truth. Brandon is hypersensitive and has deep feelings, even if he does not display them.

7. He Can Change Like the Wind but He Can Also Be as Rigid as Iron

It may seem contradictory, but in some areas Brandon changes like the wind while in other areas he is rigid as iron. For example, his food choices can change radically from one day to the next. He may love oranges today and hate them tomorrow. Sometime ago I noticed he was enjoying eating oranges, so the next time I went shopping, I bought him a bagful. To my surprise, he announced that he hated oranges, and rejected them in no uncertain terms!

On the other hand, when things change for any reason it can throw him for a loop. If a person has made a plan with Brandon, it is now carved in stone, and to change it in any way is totally unacceptable to him. If someone reneges on a plan or doesn't show up for an appointment, he could be extremely disappointed, agitated and saddened. It takes him a long time to recover and regain his confidence in anyone who has breached his trust. If it happens more than once with the same individual he will likely not want to see that person ever again. He will consider the relationship over. However, he can be more forgiving if a person who was late or failed to show up offers a sincere explanation and apology and is willing to set up another appointment right away, and then keeps it.

Brandon can tell when someone wants to be with him and when someone does not. *Over time he has grown more mature and less needy and is able to say goodbye to those who don't keep their word.* The strength he has developed in this area is one more way that he has learned to take care of himself.

Brandon is forty-one years old at this writing, and although he has been living on his own for seventeen years there are many things which are still a struggle for him. His lack of fine and gross motor skills makes it nearly impossible for him to prepare his own meals. Opening a can has always been extremely difficult for him, but just recently he was able to master using a can opener, thanks to his new Independent Living Counselor. She has been teaching Brandon how to prepare simple, nourishing meals for himself. I have tried many times, but I hope she will be more successful in this department than I have been. Besides, it's long overdue that mom stops trying to teach her son everything.

As you can see by the examples I've provided, critical aspects of your child's well-being can depend on a helper's sensitivity to your child's gray areas. For everyone's sake, be sure to write about as many as you can.

Tidbits—Nuanced Pieces of "Interesting Information"

A List of Tidbits About My Child

1. He cannot control his eating at a buffet. He will tend to overeat and get a dreadful stomachache afterward. Please do not take him to a buffet.
2. He lacks control over his fine and gross motor skills, which causes him difficulty in many areas, especially the kitchen. It is nearly impossible for him to open cans, use utensils, or cut up anything. However, he is very determined to improve as much as he can, and with practice he has been able to make some simple, adequate meals for himself.
3. Brandon likes to be treated with respect, as a peer and a friend—the same way you would like to be treated.
4. He is afraid of the flames on his stove and never uses it.
5. He always wears a baseball cap to protect his eyes from bright light.
6. On the 4th of July Brandon will likely stay at home, far away from any fireworks. He just wants the day to pass by quickly because he hates loud, unexpected noises.
7. Other holidays can pose a problem, as Brandon will often decline invitations and prefer to stay home alone. He has great difficulty with social interactions, and he does not like to change out of his usual attire of shorts and a baseball cap.

8. My son does not like to have his picture taken. If you would like to have a picture of him, ask him politely and explain why, but accept his answer if he says no. However, if he does agree to have his picture taken, be sure that you do not use a flash as it can trigger a seizure.
9. One of the more effective ways of encouraging Brandon to try something new is to first describe why *you* like it. If you start by asking him if he is interested in a new activity, chances are he will say no.

Schedules and Routines

Schedules and routines are extremely important to special needs children, especially those with autism. In your working manual you will have space to write about your child's all-important schedules and routines.

When Brandon makes a plan it is embedded in stone. You must keep your plans once you make them, and above all, be on time. If you find yourself running late, do make a point to call him on his cell phone. And always call the day before to confirm your plans.

Because my son has lived on his own for many years, I do not know his exact schedules and routines. However, I do know that having a routine is very important to him, although I must say that he has become more flexible over the years. Generally speaking, trying new things is extremely challenging for Brandon, and most often he will resist change, until he decides on his own that "it's time." This can take weeks, months, or even years.

What My Son Must Have

1. Seizure medication every day (See *Emergency Page* for more information about medications).
2. Help with his health insurance renewal every October and prescription renewals every March.
3. To be driven to the market once a month for items that he cannot otherwise carry on foot or on the bus.
4. To stay living in the same apartment.
5. Praise and kind people around him.
6. Privacy and respect (to be allowed to keep things private and to be accepted for exactly who he is).

Every November please accompany my son to buy holiday gifts for people who have helped him throughout the year. Brandon appreciates the help he gets from others, but it is very difficult for him to express how he feels verbally. A gift is a much easier way for him to say "thank you" and a good way for him to show his gratitude and appreciation without using words. The list is usually the same people, the gal who cleans his apartment, a restaurant manager, a man who owns a neighborhood jewelry store, the local police force and paramedics. These people are very important to Brandon and their continued support has helped him live the independent life that he has worked so hard to achieve.

What Works Well for My Son
1. When you call Brandon, talk for no more than 10-15 minutes, unless he has a problem that needs more discussion. You will know when he has a problem because he will obsess over it. He is usually much more talkative in the evenings, so that may be the best time to call him. Actually, any time is all right except early morning. Wait until after 10:00 a.m. to phone unless you have something urgent to tell him.
2. It is best *not* to begin a call by asking Brandon how he is doing, as he may not be able to respond adequately to this question. Rather, tell him you just called to say "hello."
3. He likes to be treated as an adult since he is an adult.
4. He needs to be driven to the market once a month to get his major shopping done.
5. He responds well to encouraging people who shower him with praise, positive input and kindness.
6. Be patient, understanding and cooperative, and communicate simply and clearly. Don't beat around the bush. Be direct.
7. Find things he enjoys. You can make a list of activities and events and see if he expresses an interest in any of them. His likes and dislikes can change quite rapidly, which can be disconcerting. An activity Brandon rejects today he could very well decide he would like to do next week.

What My Son Likes

1. Good healthy food such as salads, fresh juices, turkey burgers and chicken. As of late, animal protein in the form of chicken, turkey and fish seems to help prevent seizures.
2. To be treated to a meal at one of his favorite restaurants.
3. Baseball and basketball games, whether seeing them in person or watching them on TV.
4. Clothing made from natural fabrics which are soft, comfortable, and easy to wear. He prefers to wear shorts, even in cold weather, and seldom wears long pants.
5. To wear baseball caps from his favorite baseball and basketball teams. He always wears a baseball cap indoors and out, to protect his eyes from bright overhead lights (which can trigger a seizure).
6. Sports memorabilia from his favorite teams, the Clippers, Lakers and Dodgers.
7. A new calendar every December with pictures of professional ball players.
8. Gift cards from Trader Joe's and Whole Foods.
9. Small stuffed animals that are cute and extremely soft. However, he is very particular, so please don't be offended if your gift is not a keeper.
10. Unique watches that are durable enough to withstand a seizure.
11. Nike tennis shoes. Since he walks almost everywhere these shoes seem to hold up the best and feel the most comfortable.
12. People who make appointments with him and keep them.
13. To trust you, but it will take time for you to prove yourself and earn his trust.
14. Positive and polite people who say nice things to him and who genuinely like him. Brandon can easily tell when someone doesn't like him and is just putting up a front.
15. People with soft and gentle voices.
16. Consistency
17. Routines
18. Familiar people, places and things.
19. Independence
20. Having alone time.

21. Being treated respectfully, as an adult.
22. Peace and quiet.
23. To be himself without fear of criticism.
24. To be included and accepted.

What My Son Dislikes
1. Surprises
2. Bossy people who order him around and tell him what to do.
3. People who are rude, mean or demeaning.
4. Being asked too many questions. Sometimes one question can be too many. You will be more successful if you use a soft, gentle voice and ask him what he thinks of _____, instead of saying "I have a question for you." The former approach invites his opinion; the latter tends to put him on the defensive. The difference is subtle, but it will make a huge difference in Brandon's ability to respond.

What My Son Cannot Have or Cannot Tolerate
1. Red meat, fried foods, spicy foods, and dairy products. He can, however, have a small amount of sweets daily.
2. Nitrites and nitrates that are commonly used as preservatives in packaged meats and other food products. These substances can cause seizures. Always ask or read the labels.
3. MSG, which is used in many Asian restaurants. Always ask first before ordering.
4. Loud noises and places, bright lights and strobes (the latter can cause seizures).
5. Dark places, such as theaters or concert halls, which can also bring on seizures.
6. Having his picture taken. If a flash is used, it too, can bring on seizures.
7. He is allergic to dust and to all cleaning supplies, laundry detergents, soaps and shampoos unless they are hypoallergenic and free of all perfumes and dyes. He must use only products that are recommended by dermatologists and allergists for sensitive skin. He is not faithful to any brand and will buy whatever is on sale, as long as the packaging indicates that the product is safe for him to use.

What Makes My Son Angry, Sad, Frustrated, or Upset
1. Being asked too many questions.
2. Someone who gets too personal with him.
3. Someone who shows up late or not at all.
4. Feeling sick.
5. Being teased or made fun of.
6. Being excluded.
7. Having just had a seizure.

What Scares My Son
1. Loud noises from machinery or any unexpected, sudden noises (cars backfiring, doors slamming, loud or incessant barking, etc.)
2. Bright lights.
3. Fireworks
4. Open fires and flames on a stove.
5. Heaters and furnaces.
6. Knives and sharp objects. Due to his lack of fine motor skills Brandon is unable to safely handle anything extremely sharp. However, he is now able to use a small knife and safety scissors successfully. He is very proud of himself to have finally accomplished this task. It has simplified his life in many ways.
7. Lightning, thunder and heavy rain.
8. Screaming, hollering, arguing, and physical fighting.

My son has sensory integration issues. Even moderate light and sounds are heightened for him and are felt quite intensely. He may need to be removed from a place or situation that has caused a sensory overload. If allowed to stay in a disturbing circumstance, Brandon may experience a "meltdown."

Meltdowns most often occur when he is on overload or under great stress, which may show itself in agitation, repetition and irritation. Stop whatever you are doing and take him outside and give him a few minutes to gather himself together. You can gently tell him to just breathe and then go with him for a short walk. During this time I would recommend, you avoid talking to him unless he initiates the conversation. You will know when the meltdown has passed when Brandon reverts back to his gentle self. You can then resume talking with him in a soft, soothing voice.

Most of his meltdowns occur indoors rather than outdoors. As he has matured they are less frequent and not as long-lasting; he is able now to express what is bothering him more readily and clearly.

It's best to avoid certain situations such as large crowds, fireworks, crowded rooms, waiting in a long line, or any major stimulation. If in doubt, avoid it; it's better not to risk it.

What Not to Do
1. Do not be condescending or talk down to him like a child.
2. Do not judge him by his facial expressions. They often do not match his thoughts, feelings or moods.
3. Do not ask him a lot of questions.
4. Do not try to force him to do something he dislikes or refuses to do (unless his safety or health is in jeopardy).

Where My Son Cannot Go and Why
1. Most movie houses, concert halls, and entertainment where there are strobe lights. Darkness, noise and strobes can cause an increase in seizure activity.
2. To a buffet. He has a hard time making choices and cannot control how much he eats when there is an unlimited quantity or selection of food available. He usually becomes ill after overeating at a buffet.

Write Teaching Stories About Your Adult Child

There is tremendous value in writing short stories about your child for your networkers. Stories can paint a picture and impart a depth of understanding that cannot be achieved any other way. Writing questions and answers is another wonderful alternative to help others grasp and retain information about your child. The Q&A format is also a perfect way to express why our children do what they do. I will cover how to incorporate Teaching Stories and Questions & Answers into your manual in Chapter Six.

Sample Instructional Care Manual

Manual Summary and Overview List

This page is designed to be a quick "at-a-glance" reference for your networkers. Begin your list with the most important information you want your networkers to know and work from there. Take your time completing the list. Carefully think through each item.

Sample Manual Summary and Overview List

1. Brandon has autism and intractable epilepsy. Follow the Epilepsy Foundation's first-aid guidelines found earlier in this manual. If you are present during a seizure you will know what to do.
2. If you make a plan with my son you must keep it. If you cannot, you must call and let him know ahead of time. Changing plans for Brandon is extremely unsettling. He will also lose trust and faith in a person who makes such changes.
3. He likes to be treated as an adult.
4. Use a soft, gentle, kind voice.
5. Be positive and compliment him when you feel it's appropriate.
6. Treat him the way you would like to be treated.
7. Give him time (a minute or two) to reply when you ask him a question.
8. Call him after 10:00 a.m.
9. His cell phone number is:_____. His landline number is:_____.
10. He has great difficulty with social interactions and tends to avoid them.
11. He often does not say what he means or means what he says. It may take a while to understand this about him.
12. His facial expressions seldom match his feelings or mood.
13. He enjoys being treated to a meal.
14. He cannot eat any foods with preservatives such as nitrites and nitrates, which are widely used in processed meats. His body cannot tolerate MSG, which is often found in Asian cuisine. He has a hard time digesting red meat or dairy products.
15. He loves to eat fruits, vegetables, and animal protein such as chicken, turkey burgers and large salads with chicken. He can eat sweets on occasion, but not too many at one time.

It is often easier for people to read and retain information when it is numbered and written in short "sound bites." Be creative and explore all stylistic possibilities. One mother wrote her summary using gentle humor while another wrote her summary as a poem. Use whatever style you think will help networkers most easily understand your child. Trust your instincts.

Section 2 below will be included in your Working and Final Instructional Care Manuals located at the back of this book. I chose not to include my personal answers in these particular areas, as the information is comprehensive and would constitute a book by itself.

Section 2. Additional Pertinent Information:

- **Emergency Contact Information and Medical Care:** Physicians, Dentists, Therapists, Pharmacies, Medications, Health Conditions, Allergies, and First Aid Procedures

- **Special Dietary Needs, Meals and Food:** Dietary Restrictions and Favorite Foods

- **Legal Matters:** Attorneys, Financial Advisors, Insurance Information, etc.

- **Family Background:** Past and Present

- **School and Education:** Past, Present, and Future

- **Employment:** Past, Present, and Future

- **Residential:** Past, Present, and Future

- **Social Activities/Recreation:** Likes and Dislikes

- **Religious Affiliation:** Past, Present, and Future

- **Making Final Arrangements:** Be Prepared

- **Summary and Overview List**

In Section 2 you can write as much as you wish about each subject. The goal is to help your networkers understand your child thoroughly, easily and quickly. I will continue to provide helpful hints along the way to spark your writing and to motivate and encourage you to continue moving forward.

Notes

Notes

Five

How to Set Up Your Step-In Parenting Network

*It's not how much we give but how
much love we put into giving.*

Mother Teresa

My Friends Who Have Helped Brandon
My friends who have helped my son over the years have loved helping him. Several of them told me that although Brandon was unable to directly say "thank you" and often repeated himself incessantly, being with him made them take stock of their own lives.

They were in awe of how a man with all of Brandon's limitations was able to make it in the "real world." Spending time with him helped them put their own lives into proper perspective and made their personal challenges feel minuscule and inconsequential. After being with Brandon most of them experienced a feeling of calmness and resolve.

Those who choose to spend time with our special needs children often gain valuable insight into their own lives that they would not achieve any other way.

*It is one of the most beautiful compensations of this life that you
cannot sincerely try to help another without helping yourself.*
Ralph Waldo Emerson

Brandon gives so much by just being himself when we allow him to be. It's called *acceptance*, and is one of the greatest gifts we can give anyone. We all want to be appreciated and accepted for who we are and our children with special needs are no exception.

New Beginnings

Life has been extremely difficult for most of us over the past few years. Many people have lost their jobs, houses, just about everything during the financial crisis. With that said, I wanted to address how the past several years have impacted Brandon's world.

His support team over the years included mostly my friends. They would call him, send him cards, and take him out to do errands or treat him to a meal. Sadly, they are no longer around. Many of them moved away, or became ill, or were just too busy trying to stay afloat financially, and could no longer spend time with him.

Today, I am looking for ways to help Brandon stay on his feet and maintain his stability, and for a new group of people he can trust and want to be around. His world and his personal experiences have been shrinking due to the loss of my friends who were his helpers.

We are all asked to adjust because life is ever changing. However, for a person with autism and special needs change is difficult, if not an impossible challenge.

Brandon needs to do what we are all asked to do—to reinvent ourselves when the world around us changes. Everything was moving along so well for Brandon for many years and now his world looks and feels different, because it is. It has been hard for him to accept the changes and become motivated all over again.

He does miss his helpers, especially one gal in particular, and I am grateful that I am around and can help pick up the pieces; but I am also aware there will come a time when I am no longer here.

When Brandon's support group began to dwindle, I knew I had to make a plan to secure his future more solidly than ever. I saw what went wrong, which is why I created the Autism Independence Project and the Step-In Parenting Network program.

What is a Step-In Parenting Network?

A network is a group of helpers, hand-picked by you, with varied talents and expertise who can advocate for your child. Your network will be an informal, but interconnected group of people who are committed to help your child after you are gone, hence the name Step-In Parenting Network (SIPN). *Simply said, a networker is a volunteer helper who wishes to be of service to a special needs child when the parents are no longer able to care for their child.* These people will work pro bono. I believe if they are willing to sign up without receiving any monetary compensation they will work from their heart, because they want to, and your child will have a much better chance of receiving quality care.

My Vision for Your Network and Networkers

My vision for building your personal network is that you will have created a team to rally around your child. I chose the word "rally" because it is an upbeat word and that is how I picture your networkers. They are happy to be of service and to assist your child.

As each network is created more and more people will get involved, which will help your special needs child make his or her way in society.

Building a Strong Network

There are no real network models out there today so I am proposing the creation of an entire network of helpers. I know firsthand that you cannot put all your eggs in one basket and rely solely on one person to be there and be responsible for meeting all your child's needs in the future. *Uncertainty can cause fear and the more prepared you are now the more courageous you will become.*

Only Add People You Trust

Later in this chapter I will provide you with lists of what to look for when adding people to your network. An easy way to use these lists is to circle the character and personality attributes in a person that are most important to you. These lists have served me well in selecting good people to be included in Brandon's network. Once I meet someone in person I am better able to "size them up" and rely on my instincts to ensure that I am selecting a person that both Brandon and I will like and can trust. I would advise against adding anyone to your network that you have not met in person unless they come highly recommended by someone you respect and whose judgment you trust.

The people in my network are all quite different from one another. That is what makes it so extraordinary. These helpers will all add their own unique, positive qualities to Brandon's life—from sports, to grocery shopping, to technical support, to providing social interaction and enjoying a meal with him.

Over the coming years I will continue to fine-tune his network to make sure it runs smoothly and to make it the best it can be. *A group of solid, strong and dependable networkers with whom Brandon feels comfortable and can rely on is what I am striving to achieve.*

How Your Network Will Work

You need to know that your network is going to change over time and people will come and go. The time and chance factor is an important one, and it is critical that I make it very clear that networking is going to be a fluid and ever-changing process. While writing this book, some of Brandon's helpers have come and gone. This could be seen as a potentially daunting and discouraging aspect of the process so I will show you how to move forward in the face of these "setbacks."

Having a group of people in your network will enable it to function even if a few networkers leave for any reason. It is important that you continue to select new networkers. Right now, I have twelve people within Brandon's network, including two on a substitute list. Some of the networkers know Brandon personally and some only know about him through me.

Hopefully, when one person leaves you will have others in your network available to step in while you find a suitable replacement for the one who has left. You want to be sure to keep adding helpers, and to replace anyone who leaves, to prevent the number of people in your network from getting dangerously low. You do not want to have to scramble to add people without adequate screening because you find yourself rushed to fill a gap. You also will need to appoint a *coordinator* who will have the responsibility of managing the network after you are gone.

Ideally, the network model that I have designed will help to reduce your fears and uncertainty about your children's future. But this will only work if you are determined to take action and begin to select a group of networkers now, while you have the wherewithal. There are several key points I will cover that will help your network run more smoothly. Each network will be personalized and customized and will take on a life of its own, matching you and your child's specific needs and wants.

Tips to Help Get You Started
1. Of course, we are not about to introduce our child to everyone in our network all at one time. That would overload any child. It should be done gradually as we establish one relationship at a time, and as each individual is needed.
2. Several people in your network must be on call, willing to fill in as temporary alternates when someone leaves your network or is unable to perform his or her duties.
3. Each networker will be assigned a specific duty; some may overlap depending on your child's needs and the networker's commitment and availability.
4. Although there is a basic formula for putting together these networks, they all will be individualized and, therefore, unique. I will discuss this in more detail later in this chapter.

What all networkers will have in common is that they will be people who sincerely want to take on these positions because they want to be of service. This is your target audience and these are the people for whom you will be searching.

Although networkers are not paid I do give them small gifts on their birthdays and at the holidays to show my appreciation for their ongoing commitment to help my son. I also like to periodically send cards with something positive Brandon has said about them or something I really liked that they did for him. These small gestures seem to go a long way. We all like to feel appreciated. I want them to know how important they are and what a difference they are making in my son's life.

The Selection Process
Sharing your views and values is a must.
Initially, I never thought of Eileen as anything more than a dear friend. We've known each other for several years, and we share many of the same values. She also deeply cares for Brandon. The day I began writing this chapter

the phone rang. It was Eileen's sweet voice at the other end. I felt motivated to ask her right then if she would be willing to stand in for me and help Brandon after I die. "Absolutely!" she exclaimed. At that moment I knew in my heart she was the perfect person to add to my network.

You never know when or where you will find your networkers.

I met Eileen at a business event several years ago. She was the event photographer and was twenty-eight years old at the time. She lived close by and we became good friends. Over time I saw that many of our life values and beliefs were similar. Eileen began to feel like a daughter to me. We had an unusually strong connection from the start, a bond which has continued to grow to this day. I *trust* Eileen, which is one of my top priorities in selecting a helper for my son.

Selecting someone with similar views and values is a must. Otherwise, it will be difficult to convey how you would like your child to be treated and cared for, or for you to be confident that your wishes will be carried out. It will not work with someone who opposes you or has "ideas of their own," of which you disapprove or are wary. You want to be sure your networkers can be trusted to honor your wishes *and* will follow what you have written down to the best of their ability.

The selection process begins right where you are today, no matter how old your child is. Keep your antenna up as you go through your daily round—at doctor's offices, therapy sessions, supermarkets, drug stores, libraries, schools, meetings, restaurants, family gatherings—everywhere you go. You never know when that special person will appear.

Let's approach this search as an adventure rather than a dreaded chore. Let's step out courageously, with optimism and an open mind.

At this writing, I have twelve people who have offered to be part of Brandon's network. I will continue to add to my list as long as I am alive. People die, move away, get married, have children, or end up not having the time or desire to continue. When their plans change, so must mine. Anything can happen, and it often does.

"Be Prepared" has been my motto throughout Brandon's life. I need to be prepared now more than ever, as I diligently plan for my son's future.

As I continue to add to my list I will at some point introduce all of my networkers to one another at an informal gathering. For those who do not live close by, I will use Skype. Encouraging the networkers to get to know one another will strengthen the network and make it more secure.

Before You Begin Choosing Your Team

I strongly recommend that you do not share information about your child's finances with your networkers.

People in your network must not be involved in any way with your child's finances. I advise hiring an attorney who is well-versed in special needs trusts and financial planning to take over the responsibility of all your money matters. Save yourself time, worry, heartache, and the possibility of losing money your child needs. No one but you and your lawyer should be privy to your own and your child's monetary circumstances. It's wise to do whatever you can to safeguard your finances and prevent others from scamming or taking advantage of your child's naïvety or trusting nature. (This will be discussed at length in Chapter Nine.)

Choosing Your Team

If you can, begin by finding a team coordinator who will oversee the group and delegate tasks to the helpers as needed. Then set up your network around him or her. If you do not have someone who is willing and able to serve as coordinator at this time, don't worry. *You can start building your network today even without having a team coordinator. There are no set rules here, so feel free to be creative in building your network.* It's been my experience that when help is needed, it often miraculously appears, but of course, one must continue to take action.

I have chosen my oldest son, Matthew, as the team coordinator of Brandon's network. He knows pertinent information about his brother and will be able to answer questions from networkers that may come up or that were not addressed in the ICM. This is the perfect position for Matthew, who is dependable and capable. Other major benefits are that he is family, he knows his brother well, and loves him. I know in my heart that I can rely on him to be there for Brandon. I will talk more about siblings as networkers later in this chapter.

Never Rely On Just One Person

I did this in the past and some of Brandon's helpers became overwhelmed and burned out quickly. With a substantial network this can be avoided, but if it does happen, you will be prepared.

Let me share with you what happened while I was writing this chapter. I received a call from a wonderful networker who has been Brandon's driver for some time now. Once a month she would pick him up to do errands, and afterwards treat him to a meal. Unfortunately for us, the company she works for moved out of state and she had to relocate to keep her job. Things like this will happen and you will need to be prepared. I was very sorry to see her go and so was Brandon, but "find a new driver" has already been added to my list. I have learned that it is unwise to get attached to the idea that you will have the same networkers forever. Be aware that circumstances can change in an instant, and they often do.

Whenever one of your networkers leaves for any reason, I would suggest you have them fill out a short questionnaire to be shared with their fellow networkers. The answers will be extremely helpful for them and for you as well. These are the questions I ask those who are leaving:

1. What was your overall experience like?
2. What would you like the other networkers to know?
3. Are there any clarifications or additions you would like to see changed or added to the existing Instructional Care Manual?
4. Do you have any additional information you would like to share?

Signature: _____

Date: _____

I request that all the completed questionnaires be sent to me by email so that they are easy to read. I print them out and keep them all together in a folder with my ICM.

When I send out the questionnaire I also send the networker a handwritten thank you letter for their service.

Some networkers may still wish to continue corresponding with your child. This can be done through email, mail, Skype or by telephone.

A short questionnaire and a thank you letter will help to strengthen your network. Treat your network like one big, happy family. Listen to what they have to say and in return shower them with kindness. Keep in mind this is a team effort.

Don't be afraid to change your mind about a networker once you know more about him/her.

Recently, I found a gal who I thought would fit my criteria for a networker perfectly. After I got to know her better I was surprised to see that she lacked simple common sense and her attitude was quite negative.

I had her listed as a substitute, but removed her name from my list knowing she would not be a good fit for my son. Things like this will happen. I am happy I was able to recognize these unsatisfactory qualities in her before she began to work with Brandon. Though we may occasionally make a wrong choice, it is imperative that we recognize it and rectify the situation quickly.

Different Jobs and Duties

Each person on your networking team will have different duties to perform. Be aware of each networker's expertise and specialties and assign them tasks they are interested in and will be good at. They will be more willing to do things they enjoy and at which they excel, and will be more likely to stay with you longer. Introduce the networkers to one another whenever possible. Some of them may become friends and be able to stand in for one another if needed.

At this writing, my networkers range in age from nine to eighty-seven. The youngest is my grandson, Reed. He started out by doing very simple things, such as sending an email with a photo or a silly video to his Uncle Brandon twice a month. Even though it sounds like a small gesture, it has made a big difference in Brandon's life. When Uncle Brandon visits Reed's house, Reed helps him select and add apps to his iPad, especially games. Reed is a whiz when it comes to electronics and Brandon is not. It is a perfect match.

Reed is learning how important it is to help others. I know he has fun helping his uncle. It makes him feel important and is helping to create a strong bond between them. As Reed gets older I hope he will want to continue to help his uncle even more.

The oldest person in our network is Kenny, age 87. He is a spiritual teacher and sends uplifting cards and letters to Brandon once a month. Brandon knows Kenny and he likes him, although they have not seen each other since Kenny moved to Florida more than ten years ago. When I asked Kenny to be a networker he was delighted to have the opportunity to come back into Brandon's life through letters and cards.

To many these examples may sound trivial, but to my son they are anything but. When someone takes the time to do a seemingly small gesture, it often makes a huge impact on an autistic or special needs child. It is not how much you give but how you give.

Mother Teresa was famous for saying, "Do not strive to do great things; rather, seek to do small things with great love."

Networkers' Names

There are four men and eight women in our network: Matthew, Trisha, Sydney, Reed, Dede, Eileen, Gina, Maggie, Kenny, Lane, Lora, and Jane. I am looking to add at least one more man who is well-versed in sports. This would be a good connection for Brandon to have since he loves sports and is also very knowledgeable about baseball and basketball statistics.

I am always looking to add new people. Just the other day I received a phone call from one of Brandon's networkers. She told me she had a dear friend who wanted to sign up and be of service. She became especially interested when she found out that she would be part of a team and that there were other networkers already on board. Over the phone she sounded terrific, so I set up a time to meet her in person. If she fits the criteria I will happily add her to my list of networkers. I will then introduce her to Brandon at the appropriate time.

This is how it often works, by word of mouth. There are good people out there who really want to help. Stay open and move forward one day at a time while trusting and maintaining a positive outlook along the way.

Networkers' Duties

Many years ago it was not unusual to find families with several generations living together under the same roof. Brandon's network reminds me of those days. The only difference with his network is I get to handpick whom I want. My goal is to make it feel like one big, happy family.

I have matched each person to the duties they felt would work best for them and I will be listing them and their specific jobs. I hope it will give you some ideas and spark your creativity. Allow yourself to THINK BIG.

Finding People for Different Positions

Every child will have different needs. That is what makes this so special. You will be setting up a personalized network unique to your child.

At this time, Brandon could use help to improve his communication and social skills and to learn how to make friends and keep them. He would also like to expand his world by trying new activities, but they need to be added slowly. When I say slowly I mean *extremely slowly*. Change is very difficult for him—it agitates and stresses him out. *I learned a great tip to help Brandon's networkers:* When attempting to add anything new to his schedule, add it into the future, but not too soon. He will be more accepting if he's given a few weeks to get used to the idea. Also, clustering new activities all at one time never works—it stresses him too much and could bring on a seizure.

My son really likes it when people he knows and likes want to spend time with him. Short visits between 1-2 hours work best with him unless he is being taken on a special outing. A short text or an email can make his day.

The people listed below mostly include relatives, friends and siblings. This is a solid group of people and a natural place to begin. However, I am in the process of branching out from here and adding more people, in addition to my family and friends.

1. **Team Coordinator:** Matthew (Brandon's older brother). He is in charge of the entire network. He has invaluable information to share with others and will make all the final decisions when it comes to his brother's health, safety and well-being.
2. **Family Gatherer:** Trisha (sister-in-law). She will have Brandon come over to her and Matt's house at least once a month for a home-cooked meal. She is a wonderful cook and he enjoys going there and spending time with the entire family.
3. **Game Wizard:** Reed (nephew). At age nine he is the youngest networker. He will email his uncle twice a month to say hello and keep in touch. When he sees Brandon in person he will help him with any technical questions he has about his electronic devices—iPad, iPhone, etc., and help him add games to his iPad. He and Uncle Brandon enjoy playing games together. Reed is a silly guy with a great sense of humor and he makes Brandon laugh. That is a great gift in itself.
4. **Little Miss Sunshine:** Sydney (niece). She will call, text or email Brandon weekly to say hello and to see if there is anything he needs. If he does,

she will inform her mother, Trisha, or her father, Matthew. She is also a whiz with electronics. She is sweet, sensitive and funny, and lights up Brandon's world.

5. **Technical Support**: Lane. He will help with any technical questions Brandon may have about his electronic devices via emails or phone. He lives in the Boston area and is a teenage techie, a social media teacher, and my friend.

6. **Correspondence Gal:** Dede is a fabulous friend, organizer and editor who writes wonderful letters and emails on Brandon's behalf to insurance companies, etc. This is an area in which my son will always need help.

7. **Spiritual Teacher**: Kenny. He sends Brandon cards or letters once a month with uplifting, positive messages. Kenny, who is 87, lives in Florida and is the oldest of our networkers.

8. **Visitor:** Eileen. She is a new mom who lives 300 miles away from Los Angeles. She visits with Brandon when she comes into town, which is 2-3 times a year. She also sends birthday cards and other correspondence to him throughout the year.

9. **Telephone Gal:** Maggie is a dear friend who has a huge heart. Brandon finds talking with her over the phone once a month to be very comforting.

10. **B.E.S.T. Practitioner:** Gina is Brandon's holistic practitioner and will continue to stay in contact with Brandon and give him treatments after I am gone. To date, Gina has worked with my son for eight years and has worked with me as well. She is a beautiful, spiritual young gal and she is like family to us.

11. **Substitutes**: They will fill in the network when needed. Both Jane and Lora are parents who have young autistic children. They are also founders of two wonderful autism non-profits, Autism Long Beach and Autism Youth Sports League. They have said that if Brandon needed their help they would be there for him. As their children get older they will be more available to help out.

Four Network Positions Yet To Be Filled

On my kitchen bulletin board I have posted the following positions that need to be filled. They say if you write out what you need you will get it faster. This has served as a great reminder and in the past it has worked for me.

1. **Maintenance Person:** To help purchase hard-to-find items such as odd-sized light bulbs, hypoallergenic soaps, cleaning supplies, etc. This person will make sure Brandon avoids toxic products and has everything he needs to keep his apartment going.
2. **Sports Enthusiast:** Brandon has said he would prefer to have a man to talk to about sports and to take him to games. This is one of the best ways to quickly form a bond with him.
3. **Driver:** Someone to take my son shopping once a month for items that are too bulky or heavy for him to carry on foot or on the bus. This person may also need to be available to drive him to some of his doctor visits.
4. **Social Outings:** Someone to take Brandon out for a meal once or twice a month. This networker needs to live fairly close to Brandon. My son enjoys eating out with someone he likes and feels comfortable being with. These visits seem to work best when they are no more than 90 minutes long.

Currently, I am focusing my attention on finding networkers who live close to Brandon. I will be talking to his Service Coordinator at our local Regional Center as well as with the paramedics in his neighborhood; they have offered great suggestions in the past regarding good people who were willing to be of service.

It is a must that Brandon works with people who are kind, reliable and trustworthy. It is extremely important that he continues to be as independent as possible. These networkers are here to support my son and to make sure he has what he needs, and to cultivate his independence while giving him space to grow.

Six Important Tips When Choosing Networkers
1. Look for people of all ages.
2. Add people whom you admire, respect and trust.
3. Select people who like your child and make sure that your child likes them.
4. Always keep your antennas up and your eyes peeled. What about a neighbor, librarian, teacher, a cashier at the market, a waiter or waitress, or the owner of a restaurant you frequent?

5. Think big! Don't hesitate to add someone's name whom you think might be a good fit for your child, even if you are unsure up front whether that person will want the job.
6. Be open-minded and positive.

At first, simply start out by making a list of the names of possible networkers. Just gather the possibilities, and when you are ready, begin to talk with these people, one at a time.

If you talk with a possible networker about what you are doing and they seem interested, get them started by utilizing their services right away. Even if they start by doing something small, it is a great way for you and your child to get to know them.

Whenever you are out and the subject of networkers comes up naturally in conversation, address the issue in the moment. You may be pleasantly surprised how people respond once you speak with them. You have absolutely nothing to lose and everything to gain.

Siblings Can Often Be the Perfect Networkers, Then Again, Maybe Not

I do not feel siblings should be expected to take on the sole responsibility of caring for their special needs sister or brother unless they sincerely wish to assume that role. However, for those who want sole responsibility I would suggest that they also have a backup and set up their own network. No one knows what the future brings. As I have said before, my motto is, "Be Prepared."

When I told Matthew that I was creating a network of people to help Brandon after I'm gone, I was pleasantly surprised and relieved when he told me he thought it was a great idea, and was willing to be the team coordinator.

While writing this book I had many conversations with parents who felt that siblings would be the ideal people to step in for them. After conducting several workshops "for siblings only" I found that most of them had mixed feelings about caring for their sister or brother when their parents have passed away.

In my safe workshop environment and in private consultations *many siblings were willing to speak openly and honestly about how they would feel being the potential sole caregiver for their special needs sister or brother.* I found their comments enlightening and heartfelt and I believe you will, too.

Siblings – Comments

- I may say yes now, but I may change my mind in the future.
- Of course I will take care of my brother.
- I will do it because I must.
- I want to do it. I love my sister.
- I feel guilty and will take on the responsibility because it could have been me.
- I'm getting married and will be living in Europe and I can't move my brother.
- I will happily take care of my brother. I always expected to be his caregiver.
- I want to be free to do what I want. I'm easily frustrated and I'm afraid I'll feel burdened.
- I don't think the same way my parents do.
- It's just too much of a responsibility for one person.
- I have my own family and I will have little time.
- I will work my life around my brother.

Ask Your Child's Older Siblings If They Would Like to Get Involved

I know of families who have had siblings help in the networker selection process and it has worked out well. They were able to choose with whom they would be working and to talk with them by phone and/or meet them in person. Many siblings appreciated getting to know the people on the list and especially being included in the selection process. It is very important the siblings and networkers like one another and get along.

This may feel like a daunting task right now and it can be if you expect to find all of your networkers in one day. Take your time selecting them; over time they will appear. The selection process is exactly that—a process that occurs one step at a time.

Guardianship

If you have a guardian for your special needs child you may want to designate an alternative or standby guardian as well. No one knows what the future brings and there is no such thing as being over prepared, especially in this area. Imagine how your child's guardian would feel if he or she could count on the help and support of your group of networkers. I know it would be a welcome relief to anyone, especially when caring for a special needs child. (See Chapter Nine for more information on guardianship.)

No Two Networkers Will Look Alike

The attributes and character of a networker are essential to consider. I hope the following lists will help guide you through the selection process.

Your lists will be uniquely personal and may look quite different from mine. Feel free to include any of the attributes I've listed below that speak to you. You might want to start by circling the attributes you would like your networkers to possess.

Networkers must be willing to work with others and participate in a team setting. They must also be willing to honor your wishes and work with your child according to your outlines. Keep in mind that no one will possess all of these qualities, but the more they have the better.

The Attributes I Look For in a Networker

1. Has good reasoning skills, good common sense and good instincts
2. Is adaptable and flexible
3. Has the ability to see the big picture and recognize what is going on beneath the surface
4. Has a course of action but is able to adjust to a new one as needed
5. Has good intentions and an understanding nature
6. Is dependable and reliable
7. Is levelheaded and has a steady temperament, especially under duress
8. Possesses good problem solving and organizational skills
9. Has a caring nature
10. Is a positive thinker
11. Is practical and logical
12. Experience with special needs children is a plus
13. Knows first-aid procedures for Epileptic seizures

These Attributes Came Directly From My Heart

- Accepting
- Non-judgmental
- Willing
- Generous
- Reliable
- Emotionally available
- Positive & Upbeat
- Dependable
- Flexible
- Trustworthy
- Willing to Learn
- Easygoing
- Fair
- Understanding
- Patient
- Calm
- Neutral
- Good values
- Helpful
- Mature

Good Communication Skills

A person who communicates clearly and calmly has a better chance of avoiding misunderstandings.

Personality

I would like Brandon's networkers to be pleasant, polite, understanding, and outgoing. They will need to remain focused, but not be forceful or overpowering. They must be "present" 100% of the time while they are with my son.

Well Organized

This quality will help my son tremendously. He is a minimalist, which makes it easier for him to stay organized and keep his apartment neat. It also helps to keep his mind in order. He does not need to search for things because he always knows where everything is.

Flexibility

Brandon's moods can change rapidly from one moment to the next. The people stepping in for me must be aware of this and be able to go with his flow and stay on an even keel.

Problem Solving Skills

Good problem-solving skills and the ability to think on one's feet are a must.

Worldly Wise

Being street savvy and wise in the real-world environment, along with good common sense would be of great help to Brandon. He is quite naïve and could learn valuable lessons from a networker who has these attributes.

Sports Enthusiast

Brandon loves sports. Attending or watching games together, and sharing information and stats about the local teams is an excellent way to build and strengthen a relationship with him.

Caring

One of my top priorities is that all of Brandon's networkers genuinely care about my son and enjoy spending time with him. He knows when people are just tolerating him and when they are truly interested. This is extremely important and will make or break a relationship with him.

These are "idealistic" lists and I know most people will not even possess half of these attributes. Yet I believe you will be led to the best people out there for your child, and that they will make excellent networkers.

In the selection process broaden your views, open your heart and always be positive.

When you start preparing your list of potential networkers, brainstorm with abandon—write down every single person you can think of who might qualify. If you can only think of a few names, don't despair—even one name is better than none.

The first and obvious choices would be relatives, friends, and siblings. But if you can't think of anyone at all who would be willing and able, leave it be for now. Revisit this list from time to time and see if some names come to mind. Gathering a group of networkers is a process that takes time. Don't get discouraged. Visualize wonderful people coming into your network. Just trust! I actually had a networker's name come to me in the middle of the night.

I hope that your networkers will come together as quickly as mine did. Things fell into place once I became serious about implementing the process.

I know it might sound overwhelming and I admit at first I was hesitant about asking anyone to help. However, I was pleasantly surprised to see so many people willing to assist my son in some capacity, especially when they found out they would be part of a team. Their positive responses were encouraging and uplifting. I no longer hesitate or feel uncomfortable about approaching anyone whom I think would make a good networker.

Set Up Your Network Right Away

I suggest setting up your network right away. Why wait? Have your networkers start working with your child as soon as they have "signed on." The sooner the better for everyone involved. While you are here you will be able to help organize and orchestrate your network and get it running smoothly. This will give you the opportunity to see how it is going to work with and without you.

As you see your networkers at work, no matter how *tempting* it is, you must *resist* helping them out. Even if they take a very long time to do something, allow them to find their way unless they ask for your help. *Remember, your job is to be an onlooker and to assist when asked and to do nothing when not.* How else will they learn? This is a wonderful way to discover what areas you will need to clear up or add to your ICM. Take advantage of this incredible opportunity while you are still here.

On the following pages you will have space to write down the names of potential networkers, and a place to make notes. Remember, it will work best if you keep all of your information in one place.

List of Possible Networkers

    NAME   RELATIONSHIP   EMAIL   PHONE

1. _____
2. _____
3. _____
4. _____
5. _____
6. _____
7. _____
8. _____
9. _____
10. _____
11. _____
12. _____
13. _____
14. _____
15. _____
16. _____
17. _____
18. _____
19. _____

Notes

Notes

SECTION THREE

Helpful Stories and Answers
Every Story Has a Message and Every Questions Has an Answer

Six

Teaching Stories and Questions & Answers

We don't see things as they are, we see them as we are.

Anais Nin

Writing Stories about Our Adult Children

A wonderful way to get others to understand our adult children is by writing short stories about them. People who have read these stories have told me that they were able to understand many things about Brandon without ever having met him. Many discovered new information and ideas that they planned to implement with their own children.

It has been proven that people retain information longer when they associate it with a story or when it is in a question and answer format. Also, people seem to have shorter attention spans these days, and I have found stories that are one page or less are the most memorable.

I believe what has made the stories about my son so effective and uplifting is that Brandon himself is inspiring. He does not allow his limitations—which are many—to stop him. He is not a savant or high functioning in most areas except when it comes to numbers and managing his checkbook. He learns from experience and works hard to improve his life each and every day.

Whenever I am out speaking at conferences and parents find out that Brandon has intractable epilepsy and tonic-clonic seizures, most of them are shocked and cannot fathom how he can live by himself. They always ask me how it has been for Brandon living alone. They are usually very interested in hearing about a child who has "beaten the odds" and achieved things beyond his—or anyone else's—wildest dreams. Most parents are paralyzed by a fear of the unknown and the possible risks involved in letting their child progress to new and higher levels of accomplishment. Many have abandoned hope because they have been convinced it would be futile to try. Brandon's successes have inspired them to think "outside the box," even to ponder the "impossible." *Parents have told me they've enjoyed learning about Brandon, and were motivated by his progress over the years. I hope these stories will encourage you as well.*

The following stories are in chronological order. They depict the years Brandon has lived independently from age 24-40. I've written about bullies, girlfriends, seizures, moving, and much more. Some stories may make you squirm, and some will touch your heart, while others are sure to bring a smile to your face. Each is a teaching story with a message. These (and the many others that I have yet to write) are designed to "paint a picture" of Brandon so that those who will be helping him in the future will be better equipped to understand and aid my son.

How My Son's Journey to Independence Began (age 24)

If you were to meet Brandon on a "bad day," you might scratch your head in disbelief and wonder how I could ever have permitted him to live alone. But I knew early on that the best way to learn life is to live it.

What drove Brandon to seek independence may surprise you; it certainly surprised me. Growing up, horrific treatment from his peers made it nearly impossible for him to get close to someone his age or to anyone that he did not already know and trust. He reasoned that the only way he could be safe was to get an apartment and live by himself. He would not be subject to bullies or be told what to do and how and when to do it if he had his own home. He desperately wanted to live by himself.

In 1997 I found Brandon a small bachelor apartment in a safe neighborhood. *It was extremely difficult for me to let my son go, but I had to let him try.*

For the first several weeks, we rode the buses together until he was able to navigate the bus system on his own. We strolled around his new neighborhood until he felt comfortable walking alone. He had a job coach at his then workplace to help him with any difficulties he might face.

Though it was a huge adjustment (for both of us), Brandon took to living on his own from the very first day; he was very determined, and worked extremely hard to overcome the hurdles and obstacles he faced each day. I go into greater detail about this in Chapters Seven and Eight.

Doing the Right Thing (age 30)

This is one of my favorites.

I believe this story puts our autistic children in a positive light and shows the world some of the wonderful traits our children possess. I'm sure you have many like it, and will include them in your manual.

Brandon was working in a retail store. One day he saw something crumpled up on the floor and picked it up. He unraveled it and saw that it was a hundred dollar bill. Without hesitation, he marched into the manager's office.

"I found a hundred dollar bill and someone lost it," he announced. He handed the money to the manager and left.

Later that day one of his co-workers told him that he saw the manager put the hundred dollar bill in his wallet. Brandon responded, "I don't care, I did the right thing."

I love my son's honesty and that he does what he knows is right. He continues to be my finest teacher.

Does Your Son Have A Girlfriend? (age 34)

I am often asked if Brandon has a girlfriend. Not at the moment, but I will share a story with you about the one and only "girlfriend" he ever had.

Brandon had been seeing a girl for several weeks. I later found out she was very pretty and very young. She may have been attractive on the outside, but inside she was anything but pretty. This young gal did not have much money and wanted someone to buy her clothes, make-up, toiletries, etc. Brandon has a good heart and gave her money at first—quite a lot, in fact, but the situation started to bother him, so he went to his independent living counselor for advice. My son does not ask for help outright, and anyone who knows him well knows that certain types of statements he makes are not merely observations but are roundabout signals that he needs help. In the course of his conversation with Joe, his counselor, Brandon commented that "women cost a lot of money." If his counselor, who had been with Brandon for years, had asked, "What do you mean?" instead of agreeing with him and letting the matter drop, Brandon would have explained his dilemma and the situation could have been nipped in the bud.

Sadly, several weeks passed before he caught on that the girl was using him for his money, and that she did not like him at all. He was heartbroken. He had spent nearly $750.00 on someone who only pretended to be his girlfriend. This hurtful incident taught him to be very wary of people who ask him for money.

Although this happened to my son years ago, it upset him profoundly. He is still working on learning to trust other women. Deep down inside, though, I know he would love to have a girlfriend.

These life lessons can be cruel, brutal, and tough to get through, especially when one's child is so vulnerable. *But Brandon has always been able to learn from firsthand experience and come out on top and better for it.* I am happy to say that he learned this particular lesson well; he has not been taken advantage of in that way since.

Brandon believes that one day he will find a girl who really likes him for himself. I love his positive outlook, and hope that at the right time, the right girl will appear.

Given the Opportunity to Succeed (age 35)

I gave a speech one weekend and at the end of my talk, a gal stood up and said, "I picture your son dressed in a suit with a briefcase driving to work." I was blown away. I looked at her and said, "My son has a suit but only uses it for weddings and funerals. He doesn't own a briefcase. He has intractable epilepsy and will never drive a car." In her mind, she thought that because my son had been on his own for thirteen years, that he was living the life of a neurotypical thirty-five year old American male.

It was very important that I set her straight, and I do the same for anyone else who has misunderstood my son. Brandon has autism, intractable epilepsy, and severe learning disorders. He has enormous limitations. Every day, he has great hurdles to get over and challenges to overcome. I don't want to give the false impression that all is well with Brandon and life is easy for him. That is just not the case.

Yes, I am forever grateful that he is able to live alone. It truly is a miracle. It was also very, very hard work. I realize that it is rare for a person like Brandon to be living on his own. But if Brandon is nothing else, he is *fiercely* determined to succeed. It is this inner quality that has been his saving grace.

Food for Thought (age 36)
They say you are what you eat.

If I had to single out the best thing that happened in 2009, it would be watching Brandon mature and grow. He has reached many plateaus over the years, with long periods of stalled maturation in between. It is almost as if his mind and body need to catch up with one another periodically and get back in sync. I have realized during these seemingly dormant periods that my son is internally processing new input and information that, when integrated, bumps him up a notch.

Although Brandon has been living alone now for more than twelve years, there are many basic tasks he continues to struggle with. The most challenging has been how to eat healthfully. He has poor fine motor skills so preparing food is hard for him. Knowing what to buy to make a balanced, healthy meal—something that he will actually want to eat—is completely foreign to him.

Several months ago, Brandon and I were eating at his favorite restaurant when I realized how I could help him accomplish this most difficult task. I took a cue from the system the restaurant used. It was the type of eatery where you place your order first, then take a number and sit down and wait for your food to be delivered to your table. You make your choices from a huge glass counter filled with the day's selections. I could see Brandon was struggling with what would be best, good, or right. I asked him, "How about if you choose your food by color? Pick two bright colors, for example, the orange carrots, green beans, or yellow squash and then add one beige, white, or brown item."

Ever since that day, he has been eating much healthier. He no longer orders a sandwich with a side of fries and macaroni. His plate used to have too many starches, and looked beige, white, and grey, but today his plate looks colorful, vibrant, and healthy, and so does he. This was a huge breakthrough for him.

Brandon understands this food color concept and loves the idea. He has even taken it to the next level. When purchasing food at the market he chooses fresh salads in place of packaged items with little food value. He has replaced cookies with trail mix, potato chips with a rice snack, and his breakfast cereal is covered in rice or almond milk. He is aware that there are many healthy alternatives, and he is discovering new products each time he shops. Food shopping used to be an awful chore but now he sees it as an adventure.

Eating properly has been a huge struggle for my son. But this year he has conquered it. He is proud of himself and is able to make good, healthy choices most of the time. They say you are what you eat, and Brandon is the perfect example.

It is now a pleasure to go grocery shopping or to a restaurant with him. He knows what he wants and he has a new-found self confidence that is delightful. Eating well is now an enjoyable experience for him.

Tennis and Social Skills (age 36)

Brandon's older brother Matt moved further away and is married and has a family. He puts in long hours at work and most of his spare time is devoted to his family or catching up on sleep. He doesn't have much time to spend with Brandon these days, and consequently their relationship has grown distant. Brandon really misses his brother and could use his male companionship.

The best Matt has been able to do is to leave a voicemail message, or to send an email or text, but Brandon typically does not call back or send a reply. He does not grasp that communication goes both ways and that he needs to respond to Matt's attempts to reach out to him. Matt is hurt by his brother's lack of response and has stopped trying to communicate with him. Both of my boys are aware that their brotherly bond is frayed and that they need to reconnect, but how?

It has always been difficult teaching Brandon social skills, especially how to maintain good relationships with others. I went to sleep asking for the answer to be revealed. When I woke up the next morning I had it—tennis! I'm going to take Brandon to watch people play tennis! As a visual learner, I knew he could learn by observation how a relationship with his brother is similar to playing the game.

I took Brandon to the tennis courts where my friend John is an instructor. I told John my reason for being there, and he was happy to help. He was teaching youngsters that day and included the following lesson for Brandon's benefit.

John had a student hit the ball to him, but he made no attempt to return it. "What happens if the ball is not returned?" he shouted, loudly enough so Brandon could hear. "People lose interest in the game and want to stop playing. You cannot just stand there and do nothing. Once the ball is hit into your court, you *must* try to return it!"

I told him that is exactly what happens to your brother when you do not return his calls or respond to his emails or texts. He thinks you don't care and he loses interest in keeping up the relationship. "Matt just needs to hear from you," I said. "Remember that when you get a new message from Matt, it's now your job to send a message back as soon as you can, any way you can." "I understand, Mom," he replied.

Brandon called me the next day to say he received an email from Matt. Following my suggestion, he decided to write him a short email response, and then he called him. Matt phoned me later that day to tell me he received an email *and* a phone call from Brandon. He said that all he needed was to see that his brother was trying to keep up their relationship. He then called Brandon and made plans to take him out for dinner.

Brandon phoned to tell me how happy he was that Matt had invited him to dinner. He now understands that he must stay in touch with his brother (or with anyone else he befriends) if their relationship is to succeed. I hope he can continue to implement an appropriate response in a timely manner and that this will be a new beginning for them both.

It's a New Day (age 36)

Brandon has had to learn how to live with uncertainty. He never knows when his next seizure will occur. He has no warning, though some people do. He does not know what causes them. To make matters worse, his neurologist told us that no matter what he does and no matter what medication he takes he will never stop having seizures.

Two years ago we sought alternative treatments because we were not about to give up. Since having B.E.S.T. treatments his seizures are less frequent and less severe. I am happy to say he is making great progress. These treatments are also helping him with his social skills. (See Appendix for more information on B.E.S.T.)

Brandon has taught me how to befriend uncertainty. He has been falling down from seizures for more than twenty-seven years. When you watch someone you love fall down without any warning, you can choose to let it strengthen you or allow it to weaken you and tear you apart.

Having seizures is tough to deal with, but what makes it even worse is that a stigma surrounding epilepsy still exists. Many people believe that if you have epilepsy you are possessed by a demon or the devil. Of course, we know that is not true, and I do what I can to educate people.

The beauty of this story is my son has such a wonderfully positive attitude. He is not burdened by what happened yesterday, or the day before. He lives in the present. Even after having a seizure, the next day he is up and raring to go. When I ask him how he feels, he always replies, "Mom, it's a *new day.*"

A Near Restaurant Fiasco (age 37)

Last week, I was out having lunch with Brandon. We were at a self-serve restaurant inside a market. We split up; I went to the food section and Brandon went to get napkins and silverware and secure a table for us.

When I glanced his way I saw him standing in front of the silverware dispenser, anxiously pressing the red arrow that pointed to the handle that you push to retrieve a utensil. When this didn't work, he tried to pull off the top of the machine, but it would not budge. He abandoned that one and moved to the machine next to it and tried to pull the top off of that one, too. By now he was extremely frustrated.

An alarmed cashier, who thought he was trying to vandalize the dispensers, ran over and demanded to know what Brandon thought he was doing. Even from a distance it was obvious to me that he was not deliberately trying to break the machines. I rushed over and intervened, explaining the situation to the cashier as calmly as I could. My first attempt to show Brandon how to use the machine failed, as he was still hyper-focused and stuck on pressing the arrow. After a few more tries, though, he finally got it. What a relief!

I gently explained to him that this kind of thing happens to me, too. When I'm traveling on business and I'm at a new airport, and especially if I'm tired, I sometimes have trouble getting vending machines to work. Sharing my own experience in a soothing tone helped ease Brandon's frustration. It also helped him learn that he was not the only one who had problems with pesky machines.

Brandon has had to learn many lessons and negotiate living in the "real world" largely on his own. What I love most about my son is that he is determined to learn, and he does not brood over the past. He truly knows how to live in the "now." (I repeat this throughout the book because it is an attribute that has made my son's life so much better, as it would anyone's life.)

Bullying, Options, and Choices (age 37)
I assumed he knew this, but I was wrong.

Brandon was being teased and bullied by a group of adults in his neighborhood. It took several weeks for him to tell me what was happening, but he finally told me about it, because it was out of his control and he did not know what to do.

Over the years, I have had to become a detective to find ways to extract the information that I needed from Brandon in order to help him. I have learned what to ask and how to ask it so I can get to the bottom of an issue. I have had years of experience doing this and today it comes quite naturally.

This time, the initial question that uncovered the problem was, "Do these people hang out in the same place every day?" When Brandon said yes, I asked why he kept going back there if they treated him so badly. He said, "They told me I had to come back." He looked at me as if to say, "You mean I have a *choice?*"

My heart sank. My son obviously was not aware that he had the choice to avoid a place he did not want to be. He did not know he had the right to walk away if he was being hassled. I wondered if he just wanted to fit in so badly that he felt being bullied was better than not having any friends at all.

We spent the next several minutes talking about having choices and what that meant to him. We also talked about his rights. We had talked about all of this before, but he never related it to being teased and bullied, and so he was unable to access the information when he needed it most.

After our talk, in which I explained that he could walk a different way to avoid that corner where the group hung out, he never returned to that street corner again and was no longer bullied by those men.

I know I cannot assume anything when it comes to Brandon. It is necessary to cover all the bases and to make sure he knows he always has choices. He cannot be given *too* many options, though, because it will put him in overload. I always have to be aware of the delicate balance between "not enough" and "too many." For now, though, having two choices seems to be the magic number.

I have found the best way to reach my son is to address him respectfully. Brandon responds well when he is treated well. Don't we all?

Making time to be available and having simple, basic talks with our adult children, rather than approaching a teaching moment like an inquisition, can encourage them to open up.

As a Mom I Continue to Learn (age 37)

Yesterday, I met Brandon for lunch. It was a sizzling,105-degree day. Most people I know don't like it that hot and Brandon and I are among them.

When he got in my car he could not stop talking about the heat and how hot he was. He was dressed in a pair of shorts and a light short-sleeve shirt, with a heavy, hooded winter sweatshirt tied around his waist.

I said, "Brandon, you might want to take off your sweatshirt. It's heavy and is causing you to feel even warmer." He said, "Mom, don't tell me what to do. I am not a baby." He gave me "the look" that said, *"Leave me alone."* I didn't say another word about the sweatshirt until he repeated how he hated the heat at least twenty-five more times. "Brandon," I said, " if you can't stand the heat any more, try taking off your sweatshirt and see if it makes a difference. You can always put it back on." He shot me another "look," and begrudgingly took off his sweatshirt. After a while he admitted that taking it off made him feel "a little cooler."

Lying in bed that night I pondered why Brandon was so unwilling to give up his sweatshirt. Then it hit me! He always has a sweatshirt with him because down by the beach where he lives, the temperatures can fluctuate dramatically. He likes being prepared, so if he's out and the weather changes suddenly, he always has his sweatshirt handy to keep him warm.

As you can see, even after being on the special needs path for more than thirty-seven years, *I am still learning.*

Keeping Our Children Safe (age 38)

Most people who have autism and special needs are easy prey. They are usually naïve and trusting, and unprincipled people are often able to take advantage of them. In today's world we have to be more careful than ever to protect our children, especially our children with special needs.

Even though my son is a grown man, he still continues to be bullied and taken advantage of by other adults, which shocks and troubles me. One would hope that people would grow out of this immature, obnoxious behavior.

However, as you know, if we live out in the "real world" bad things can happen; none of us is guaranteed a safety net.

I often spend time helping Brandon recognize that he has choices, and I share anecdotes with him about staying safe. If I don't lecture him, but engage him by telling "stories," he is more apt to listen and is able to digest what I am trying to get across. I also use positive reinforcement rather than scare tactics.

Just last week, Brandon sold his newly-purchased cell phone to a so-called, "friend." The man told him that he would pay him $200 later (much less than Brandon had originally paid for it), and he would add him to his calling plan for only $20 a month. He believed and trusted this man until he found out that the man left town in a hurry and disconnected his cell phone. Brandon of course had no way to get in touch with him to collect his $200. In addition, he had to pay extra money and work very hard to try to recapture his old phone number and open a new account.

Brandon finally realized and sadly admitted the man was not really his friend. Yes, my son lost $200, but I believe he learned a valuable lesson.

Of course I am not happy that he lost $200. Who would be? However, I am grateful that the man did not try to physically steal the phone off of Brandon and harm him in the process.

I have been asked to teach workshops on safety for parents who have children with special needs. Yes, to protect them we often must be extra-vigilant, but I also believe that it is important not to let fear prevent us from allowing our children sufficient freedom to experience life. *Each of us needs to find that happy medium where our children can be as safe as possible as they find their way in the world and grow into their full potential.*

My motto when it comes to safety is: Be courageous, trust, continue to educate yourself and your child. Think positive and be knowledgeable, and stay up-to-date with what is going on in your neighborhood and the surrounding communities.

Don't forget to talk openly about bullying. But please do not scare your children, inform them.

What I Discovered Along the Way (age 38)

It is hard to believe that Brandon recently celebrated his thirty-eighth birthday. We have been through many ups and downs together. Countless times I felt beaten down and wanted to give up, but my love for my son kept me going. Brandon has taught me so much. ***These are just a few of the wonderful lessons I learned from my son:***

- Parents set an example by their actions, not their words.
- I must not allow my fears to become my son's fears.
- Remember to pause, breathe, and regroup throughout the day.
- Celebrate each person's uniqueness.
- We all have choices and we must choose our options wisely.
- Taking care of yourself first gives you the strength to carry on.
- Encouraging words help to build self-esteem.
- Live in the moment rather than the future in the "what if" zone.
- Being kind will open more doors for my child and me.
- I don't have to listen to negativity.
- I can trust myself and my instincts.
- I must be willing to be flexible and change my ways.
- When I replace the word "worry" with "wonder" I see life from a more positive perspective.
- When I allow myself to surrender, acceptance follows.
- Love and support will help to build a strong foundation in any home.

Today, I cannot thank my son enough for silently demanding that I grow and change every step of the way. He helped me to see life though his eyes and taught me to believe in myself and to be more creative, kind and courageous. Yes, it took a long time for me to see the good and to be able to switch from being negative to being positive. However, when I surrendered and was able to accept my son just as he was, I became a more compassionate and loving mother.

Are You Moving or Staying? (age 39)

Brandon has hit many bumps in the road and faced many obstacles over the past fifteen years. But nothing prepared either of us for what was about to happen.

Brandon has been living in an apartment near the beach for the past seven years. He loves where he lives. He and I expected him to live there until the end of his life, but then the unexpected happened. The city decided to demolish the seven-story parking structure that is attached to Brandon's apartment building and erect an eleven-story parking structure in its place. It will take approximately two years to be completed.

The noise from the jackhammers and the other heavy-duty equipment was excruciating for Brandon, who has serious sensory issues. Incessant loud noises like this make him a candidate for frequent seizures.

Brandon was getting ready to see if he could work again with Best Buddies (see Appendix) and find a new job. However, with the shaking and the vibrations from the demolition, he began to experience multiple seizures each day for several weeks. This was a completely new and dreadful experience for him.

How was I going to help my son cope with the noise? Was moving the only viable option? I asked him what he disliked more, all the loud noises or moving to another place to live? "I hate them both," he answered.

Later, Brandon called to tell me he didn't want to move. I took that with a grain of salt, as he is prone to changing his mind from day to day. I know how extremely hard this must be for him. It's been difficult for me to watch him endure this. I tried to explain to him that making a firm decision about moving or staying is a process. I told him that some days he will want to move and other days he will want to stay. He was very confused because he couldn't make a decision and stick with it.

This is really tough. All I can do is be there to support him while this demolition and rebuilding persists. His counselor from the Regional Center is looking into a volunteer job for Brandon which will help to keep him away from the noise at least part of the day. I am trying to find something for him to do during the day as well when the noise makes it impossible for him to stay in his apartment.

Many people have asked me why I don't have my son move in with me temporarily. I live in a tiny bungalow that is at least forty minutes away from Brandon's apartment. It would very difficult for him and would set him back to have to start all over again and get acclimated to everything new. What is most important, though, is that he is not interested in moving away from the area he knows and loves. He has chosen to find ways to tough it out.

Just when you think you have weathered the worst of times, things like this appear. It is inevitable when one is living life. Problems will crop up. We cannot assume we will be spared from the everyday challenges that occur. *What better way to learn life than through living it?*

Preyed Upon Yet Again (age 39)

Last week, I went over to Brandon's to take him to do errands and treat him to lunch. The street was very crowded as we walked toward the car. There were people everywhere. Among them was a man who seemed to know Brandon and was making a beeline for him. He raised his arm as if to slap Brandon, who swiftly and intuitively moved to the curb. This threw the man off balance and he tumbled to the ground. We managed to get to the car without further incident and drove away.

Although it all happened in a split second, it was obvious that the man knew Brandon and posed a threat to him. When I asked him who the man was, he vehemently denied knowing him. I thought it wiser not to pursue the matter just then, but I would have to discuss the incident with Brandon at some point. When I brought it up at lunch, he still refused to talk about it. However, later that afternoon he admitted that he knew the man, whom he described as a "big troublemaker."

It is most disturbing and unfortunate that things like this still happen to him from time to time. Being bullied, teased and picked on has been a challenge for him most of his life. I was amazed to see Brandon respond so quickly and instinctively to avoid getting assaulted. My son was developing "street smarts!" This is yet another example of how he has been able to learn from life by living life.

Would I Choose the Same Path Again? (age 39)

I was speaking at a conference and at the very end of my speech I told the audience "I would choose this same path again." A mom in the back demanded to know why.

I stood there frozen while my mind raced through Brandon's life, from his birth to this moment as an adult. It happened in a flash.

I replied, "It has been a very difficult path. I can't deny that. But while helping my son I was also helping myself. Most of the time, though, I was unaware of this. The path has been extremely tough but it is one that is also rich with treasures if you are open to seeing them."

Quite frankly, I would never have stayed the course if it were not for the fierce love I have for my son. This path was and is tough, but the rewards for me have been tremendous. I am forever grateful to Brandon; through him I have found my calling—speaking, writing, and helping others along the special needs trail. I know that I must walk my talk. I must be a shining example and continue to learn and grow just as my son is doing.

Six of the Most Important Lessons I Learned Along the Trail:
- My way is not the only way.
- Flexibility is the secret to staying young.
- Being unique can be beautiful.
- Listen to what people have to say, but know that they often speak most loudly when they are silent.
- We are all doing the best we can. If we could do better we would.
- Find something good in every negative situation.

The Dance of Independence (age 39)

When I was an adult, my mother shared a story about me when I was four years old. I was the youngest of three girls. One day while my mom was pushing me on a swing in the park, I told her to stop. "I can do it by myself!" I declared. My mother stopped, and when she backed away from the swing she began to cry. "My baby is growing up and she does not need me anymore," she said to herself. She told me it was one of the saddest days of her life.

I never understood how she felt until recently, when Brandon did something similar. When I called him a couple of weeks ago he rudely demanded to know what I wanted. He clearly was irritated and responded to everything I said with, "Yeah, yeah, yeah." To make matters worse, he has kept this up for more than a week now.

At first, I was offended and a wave of sadness poured over me. Then I realized that he was trying to tell me he needed more space. But because he has difficulty expressing himself verbally, this was the best he could do.

Then it hit me like a ton of bricks. My son, whom I have spent thirty-nine years teaching how to become ever more independent was now showing me that all my efforts were finally paying off. I have to give Brandon credit because it took a lot of courage for him to speak out even if he was unable to express himself clearly or kindly. We all have to start somewhere.

Once again, I was being asked to "let go," this time more so than ever. Brandon wanted to move to another level of independence, just like I was, all those years ago on the swing. Yes, I was four then, and Brandon is thirty-nine, but it does not matter how long it takes, as long as one continues to progress, one day at a time.

Independence is like a dance; actually, it is like many different dances. You always need to be asking yourself, "What tune is playing?" Is it a waltz, a quick step, or the funky chicken? Knowing the correct tune makes a huge difference. It helps you to know when to step in and when to step out.

I realized I was dancing to the wrong tune, an old tune. I knew I needed to back up and give my son more space; he would eventually come around. He did, and shortly thereafter we were able to start discussing when he feels he needs me and when he does not. I can see that this, too, will be a process, much like everything else.

The reason I felt it was important to include this story is that sometimes we are not aware that our child is changing or growing. We miss the signals. Even when we do not see dramatic changes or maturation for long periods, we must not give up. As you can see, Brandon's development, though often subtle, continues on. We must love, support and teach in a kind way and step in and out to the tune that is playing at any given time. (I talk all about "letting go" in Chapters Seven and Eight.)

Still Changing After All these Years (age 40)

One of the most important aspects of Brandon's willingness to change is that it is happening more and more as he ages. That goes against most findings from doctors and specialists in the field of autism and disabilities. That is why I continue to talk it up. I want to bring you hope for your child's future. Hope is something we parents never seem to get enough of.

At the beginning of Brandon's journey to independence he had new tasks and many daunting issues to deal with every day. I never knew what the next one would be. Now, at this writing, he has been living independently for seventeen years, and I am thrilled to report that most days Brandon has good things to say about his life. He continues to change in areas which have stalled him for years.

Listed below are just a few of these amazing changes:
1. He is willing to make a doctor's appointment for his yearly physical and not complain about having to go or to be reminded.
2. He has fruit in the house in place of candy and sweets. He eats more salads and vegetables and less processed fast food. He enjoys eating more healthfully; he says it makes him feel better.

3. He is able to wait a year for his cell phone contract to expire and get a new phone and not constantly talk about it like he used to. It used to be a daily issue but not anymore. He told me that he was fooled into signing a two-year contract. So we went over what his choices will be when he gets his new phone. Next time he will be prepared and will get exactly what he wants.
4. He is often able to show appropriate feelings and connect the feelings to actual situations that occur. He is able to apologize and say "thank you" and "your welcome" at the proper times.
5. He is more able and willing to change, adapt and step out into new territory and try new things. This is HUGE!

I hope these stories encourage you to never give up. We don't know when or how much our children will be able to grow and change. But what we do know for sure is that it will be at their own rate and in their own time, rather than ours or anyone else's.

By learning you will teach, by teaching you will learn.

Russian proverb

I understand everything Brandon says and does even if it sounds or appears weird to others. He needs to be respected for exactly who he is and not be forced to change. His unique way of being and viewing the world have made him the man he is today.

I have learned to allow my son the comfort of his ways no matter how odd they may appear to me or to anyone else. My motto is simple: "If Brandon is not hurting anyone and he is not getting hurt, just let him be."

How I would like people to treat my son:
- To guide, not force
- To instruct, not insist
- To demonstrate, not demand
- To suggest, not "should"
- To walk one's talk and to be a good example
- To offer him a few choices and options along the way

- To treat him exactly the way they would like to be treated
- To speak to him respectfully and treat him as a peer

Many autistic adults appear naïve and immature. But often that is not actually the case. Just as you cannot tell a book by its cover, you cannot always tell what an autistic adult is thinking, or what their capacity is to understand what is being said. Although many of our children are not able to express their feelings in the moment, or are able to stop the conversation when they've heard something that bothers them, they have the same feelings as everyone else. They need to be given the chance to respond in their own way and at their own pace. I like to apply the "60 second rule." I wait 60 seconds, and if Brandon has not responded to what I've said, I will ask him if he has heard me or I will repeat myself again. I wait patiently for him to reply.

These stories were written especially to help networkers learn how to reach out and interact appropriately with my son, and to bring hope and information to parents, too.

Questions and Answers

Firsthand Experiences are Priceless

Obtaining information from people who have had firsthand experience is worth its weight in gold. I recommend that you find adults you respect and admire who have faced some of the same challenges your child has, and ask for their input and advice.

You will want your networkers to be able to access important information about your child quickly and easily. I believe the following Q & As will do just that.

Let Me Introduce You to My Friend, Rory

I asked my autistic friend, Rory, who is in his sixties, to address many of the questions I have had about my son. I also asked him questions about his life in general. I found his answers to be enlightening. I learned more about why Brandon does what he does in the few minutes I spent reading Rory's words, than I had in the previous ten years.

His answers are interesting and informative and are a fabulous way for Brandon's networkers to understand him more easily, clearly and quickly. This is exactly what you will be striving to accomplish for your networkers as well.

Rory: "I was in my fifties before I was diagnosed with Asperger's. Although I had been odd all my life no one had picked up on it. It is a struggle for some people with Asperger's to live independently. I cheated and married a wonderful woman who handles the world for me.

"I have been married now for more than thirty years, and I am a father and a grandfather. I have been in full-time employment most of the last thirty-six years. The intervening period between the discipline I was under at school and getting married was filled with a series of, let us say, embarrassing misjudgments. I have difficulties navigating the world by myself and marriage has enabled me to lead a normal life. I am not suggesting that all people with Asperger's need to marry, but I do believe they need some sort of support structure.

"For many people with Asperger's their primary support is their parents, and for many of those parents like Amalia Starr the question has to be faced, "What happens to my son when I am no longer here?" More and more of us are becoming adults with Asperger's, which is why the efforts of people like Amalia, who are discovering the secrets of independent living for people with Asperger's, are so important, and why the experience of adults with Asperger's is so vital to that quest."

I have never met Rory in person but through social media we became friends. I adore him and I truly appreciate his willingness to be open and take the time to answer the following questions. I found his wisdom and firsthand experiences to be invaluable, and I hope you will as well.

1. **What are services like in Scotland where you live?**

Sadly, facilities and support for people with autism and their families varies greatly from place to place. I live in Glasgow, which has an Autism Research Centre as well as a branch of the National Autistic Society, and facilities like East Park Home. But there is always more that could be done. Some areas are badly served. A recent report showed in some parts of Wales children are waiting up to seven years for a diagnosis. Given how important early intervention can be, no child should have to wait that long.

2. **What do you want people to know about you and about autism?**

I grew up not knowing I am autistic, so I had no choice but to make a go of things. I am in many ways high functioning. Sadly, I don't have any special gifts, but many people with Asperger's syndrome don't. I would like people to know that given support, autistics can have fulfilling lives. Some may not achieve independence, but in many (I believe most) cases improvement is possible.

3. **If you could say anything to neurotypical people, what would you say?**

I would adopt the title of one of the National Autistic Society's campaigns, "Don't Write Us Off." Looking at autistics from the outside you will form impressions of what our lives are like, and how we feel. Please remember we are not you. Listen to us and support us. Look at people like Carly Fleishman; when she gained access to a keyboard she demonstrated that instead of being retarded she is an intelligent young woman well able to express herself!

4. **What is it like to have Asperger's?**

What's it like to be neurotypical? I don't really have a point of comparison. I'm just the way I am. Autism is a spectrum, and Asperger's is a spectrum within a spectrum. I feel very much like an alien trying to make sense of a world in which I don't really belong. These days people are making an effort to explain the unwritten rules of societal behavior, but when I was growing up, I think my overriding sensation was one of perpetual confusion. My attempts to understand the concept of romance have provided my wife with hours of amusement.

5. **How do you feel in social situations?**

To be honest I prefer not to be in social situations. I can handle a small group where I know everyone, and I can handle a crowd where no one knows me, but interactions can be agony. I find it difficult to follow conversations if there are any distractions because I tend to hear everything at once and cannot separate one input from another. When I was a child at parties I used to find a quiet place and read.

6. What will happen to our adult children if they cannot socialize and cannot pick up on social cues?

They will be like me, and what's not to like? Seriously, they will find social situations agony, but there are rules to follow which make a fair amount of interaction possible. These will not always work and there will be moments of hideous embarrassment, misunderstandings, alienated friends, and times they will want the earth to open up and swallow them. I'm sorry, but that's how it is. On the other hand, they will learn the sort of social interactions that do work for them and may well develop a small circle of friends who appreciate them as they are and see beyond their social maladroitness. Some of these people, too, may be odd!

7. How can we help our children fit into society? They want friends, but have a very hard time making and keeping them.

Firstly, I think parents should remember that their child's needs may be different from theirs and that the level of social interaction you need may be insufferable to them. That having been said, they may require a degree of social interaction and it is possible to support them. I am fortunate in being a child of the 1950s when codes of social conduct were rigid. I think formal manners properly explained make social interactions easier. I feel sorry for today's children.

8. Many of our adult children lose their jobs due to the inability to socialize and communicate, even when they are able to do the tasks. How can we help them?

The short answer is, provide them with opportunities, not pressure. We can flourish in the right environment, but we do need to have a degree of control over it. We should be allowed to socialize on our own terms; forcing us into situations in which we experience discomfort is more likely to damage others' opinions of us and our ability to socialize. With practice we can learn to handle challenging situations, and I frequently (although that is a subjective opinion) step out of my comfort zone.

I firmly believe that there is little point in trying to conceal one's autism; it is better to allow people the opportunity to understand one's unusual behaviors.

By being up front it also allows one to discuss with employers the adaptations which will allow them to get the best value from one.

9. If you have autism, is loneliness an issue?

I have on occasion, mostly as a child, felt somewhat excluded because I had no idea how to fit in. I rarely feel lonely now because I am used to spending most of my time on my own. I have a job which provides me with rather more human interaction than I like. Because I am married and have an attentive family, I am never allowed to be alone for long.

The greater problem is the sense of isolation I can feel when with others because so much of what is happening escapes me. Even in a room full of people it feels as if I am looking in through a window.

10. How can we better understand our autistic children and adults?

I wonder whether you can. I think this sort of exercise where you actually ask us how we think and feel, rather than making assumptions based on your way of thinking and being, is a great start. There are an increasing number of autistic people writing about their experience of life and some, like the redoubtable Temple Grandin, who speak in public. However, autism is a spectrum and no two of us are the same, but there is such a level of overlap in our experiences that wide reading will give a degree of access to most of them.

What you may never get is how the actual experience feels, and understanding why an action produces a particular result may be as much a mystery to me as to you, the observer. No one can truly know what it is to be another, so be open to the autistic, ask questions, but don't push too hard.

11. How can we tell if our children are happy? They often lack facial expressions.

I always say that, "in the absence of evidence to the contrary assume I am happy." Sometimes, thankfully rarely, I experience savage depressions that can last for months. They take me by surprise, because in reality I don't process feelings all that well, except at the extremes. Most of the time I feel reasonably content, even when people around me are upset or howling with laughter.

To be perfectly honest I'm not great with facial expressions although I have learned several. I have discovered that the emotions people feel are not always those I would expect looking at their faces. I think it's probably fair to say that our facial expressions are generally honest if not always expressive.

12. Why does my son have a sad or negative tone to his voice? When I ask him if he is angry or sad he says he is neither.

The tone you hear in your son's voice exists in your interpretation. I think with someone with Asperger's you need to listen to the content of their speech rather than the tone. My tone, like your son's, sometimes has people asking me what is wrong, when I am perfectly ok. It is not consistent.

13. Why is it my adult child will not say "thank you", "you're welcome", etc.?

I have this same problem. In fact, it was this that first led to me being sent for diagnosis, as it was causing some problems at work. In my particular case the primary problem was an inability to use the forenames of people to whom I had not been introduced. I could never understand why I should say "sorry" when I wasn't, or "thank you" when I didn't feel gratitude. I have no difficulty using the terms when they are appropriate, but I find it impossible to use them as a convention, to do so deprives them of any value.

14. Some days my son looks as though he has it all together. Other days it seems that he can barely make it out in the world.

I think we all have days like that. Much of the time I am together, but some days, for no reason I can perceive, my tics are worse, I stim more, and I am more than unusually sensitive to noise and light. On those days everything becomes a struggle, and it takes much longer to understand what is happening and what people are saying. If I were to say I knew the answer I would be lying, but my best guess is, if it starts in the morning, it would be either some sort of chemical imbalance or perhaps an adverse reaction to a dream. Later in the day, it perhaps is caused by an overload of stimuli. In all honesty I don't know why it happens, but it does.

15. Can you tell me why my son's schedule is set in stone?

Speaking for myself, having a schedule makes the world more manageable. Knowing *what* is going to happen *when* avoids the difficulty of processing the unexpected. I have real difficulties when, for example, my wife has said she will cook one thing and then changes her mind. I have been known to cook the original dish for myself so that my expectations are satisfied.

16. How can we help our autistic adults have a good life?

Remember we are adults, however childlike we may appear. Just because we appear innocent, perhaps a little slow, does not mean behind the facade there is not a formidable intellect. We may see things differently from you, but we are adults and many of us have the same concerns as any other adult. Many autistics want the same things as you—jobs, status, relationships, but we may possibly understand them differently. Be patient, and explain the things that may not occur to us. For example, I wanted my own business, but it never occurred to me there would be paperwork involved. We may need prompting to think things through. However good we are at processes, we may need to be made aware that we need one.

17. What about self-advocacy?

We can in many cases speak for ourselves; even the non-verbal may use a keyboard (no one can convince me Carly Fleishman can't speak for herself). However, there are circumstances that militate against us. We may not process language quickly enough to argue a case in real time; we may find problems with the environment; we may take statements at face value and accept untruths because, to be honest, it does not occur to us that public servants would lie if employed to provide a service to the public.

18. How is it that my son does not carry old baggage into the next day?

I think you may find that he has a physical memory rather than conscious one. I too drop the past very easily, but some physical stimuli when repeated provoke the same physiological reaction as on previous occasions.

19. Why do our autistic children take everything literally?

Words have defined meanings; we determine the meaning of a sentence by the content of the words it contains and the context in which it occurs—that's logical. At school I used to love analyzing sentences. If meanings are blurred it is very confusing. I think digitally and can only appreciate the nuances of analogue thinking by subjecting it to analysis. We take things literally because it is too painful and time consuming to do otherwise.

Mission Accomplished!

Thank you, Rory. I am sure that networkers and parents will find your answers incredibly helpful, interesting and informative, just as I have.

As I close this chapter, I will be featuring a final teaching story, thanks to a mom who heard me share it at an autism conference. She felt all special needs parents would benefit from this information and asked if I would include it in my book in a prominent place.

Keeping Your Child Safe

All special needs parents worry about their children's safety. For the past several years there have been disturbing stories on the news and social media about autistic children who have been misunderstood and mistreated by law enforcement. What can we do to help keep our children safe? Let me share with you what has worked well for my son, which I believe will work for your child, too.

Brandon has gravitated to policemen and firemen since he was a young boy. When he moved into his new apartment six years ago, there was a police substation located next door. Brandon would go in there daily and talk with the officers. They took a liking to him, and he told me that he felt safe when he was with them. He considered them to be his friends. He even gave the officers an extra key to keep for him in case he ever lost his.

In Brandon's neighborhood there are officers walking on foot, some are on horseback, while others ride bicycles, and they also cruise around in standard patrol cars. They are everywhere and are "intentionally" visible. When they see Brandon they go out of their way to say "Hi." He likes the recognition and will often stop and talk with them. If Brandon has a problem, he will tell them. If they know about an incident in the area that he should stay away from, they will inform him. Brandon told me that often a policeman will tell him when to go home at night. He said, "Mom, I listen to them because I know they care about me. Now I know when it's time to go home; they don't need to tell me."

After seeing how well this was working for my son I made a visit to his local fire station to talk with the paramedics and give them a copy of my first book, *Raising Brandon*. In it I had written, "If you assist Brandon during a seizure, when it is over and if he is not injured, please take him home instead of to the hospital." They have been honoring my wishes for the past six years, which has made Brandon's life so much easier. They watch out for Brandon and take the time to talk with him. Many will address him by name when they see him walking around town.

I suggest making an information sheet for the paramedics to keep on file. Attach a photo and include your child's name, age, and anything you feel they should know about your son or daughter.

I also suggest paying a visit to your local police station and introducing yourself and your child to whomever is on duty. Tell them about your concerns and how your child might respond if there were to be an interaction with law enforcement. Share important information about your child that would be considered unusual behavior, such as being a wanderer or runner; is he/she non-verbal or does not speak much; does your child make odd movements accompanied by odd sounds, is easily frightened, or when told to stop is likely to continue running, etc. This is crucial information that will help the officers better understand your son or daughter so that if there is a need to approach or interact with your child, they will understand his/her behavioral tendencies and react appropriately.

Plan to visit the police station at least a few times a year. Who knows, maybe your child will like going there as much as my son does. Go on a different day each time you visit so that you can meet new officers and give everyone you can the opportunity to get to know your child.

It is also important to keep tabs on any changes in these departments that may affect your child. For example, I need to go back to the fire station soon and let my wishes be known again because recently there has been a huge turnover in personnel.

Having these face-to-face interactions with the paramedics and police officers and giving them information to keep on file could one day save your child's life, no matter what age your child is. The more people in the community who know and understand your child, the better; it will also go a long way to ensure your own peace of mind.

SECTION FOUR

Independence

Independence Training for Parents is Essential

Seven

How to Prepare You and Your Child for Independence

Every morning we are born again.
What we do today is what matters most.

Siddhartha Gautama

Wherever You Are Today Is Where You Need to Begin

Parents are always asking me how I helped my son become independent. This chapter is devoted to answering that question and much more. Achieving independence is a step-by-step lifelong process. It never ends until you leave the planet. However, it does get easier over time.

Most parents of special needs children become overprotective, and rightly so.

This chapter is filled with tips and strategies that will help you overcome your fears, anxiety, overprotective tendencies, and learn the art of "letting go." What you do today to help your son or daughter reach independence will help your child for the rest of his or her life. I hope you will read through these pages with an open mind and choose the tools that will work best for you and your child. Begin by taking action and implement them right away.

Your beliefs and thoughts are exactly that, only yours. It is crucial to be broadminded and be willing to learn, understand, and accept the way your child thinks.

Fear can and does stop parents from letting go of their adult child, which limits the child's opportunities for achieving independence. I want to share a short story about a woman I met on the Internet. She had a fourteen-year-old son who had autism. He was high functioning in many areas. She and her husband and son lived in a small town. Everyone knew her son and the town felt like a safe place to live. When she learned that my son was living alone and had been for the past seventeen years her response was, "It is such a lonely life to live alone."

I never thought of my son as being lonely; instead, I thought of him as being peaceful. The following day I called and asked Alfonso, Brandon's Service Coordinator at the Regional Center, to see if he felt that my son was lonely. I just wanted to make sure that I wasn't missing something. He said, "No I think he's happy living by himself. At least that's how it appears to me." That is how I see it as well.

I wanted to include this story because no matter how long we have lived we parents have our own limited experiences and views. It is extremely important that we do not allow our own limitations and fears to become our child's.

I have had to continually change my views and rearrange my limited thinking along the way to allow and help my son to live on his own. Although I have lived a long time, my experiences are just that, they are only mine. My son has had his own experiences and he has grown from them. Without them he would not have learned how to manage his own life as well as he does today.

I received a phone call recently from a gal who wanted to hire me as a speaker at her upcoming event. She asked me how I was able to help my son achieve independence. She seemed to think I had a magic potion or I did it by waving a magic wand. I told her that there are no magic potions and I don't have a magic wand, but I sure wish I did.

Achieving independence requires love and patience and is a process that occurs over time.

After I accepted my son for exactly who he was Brandon led the way. Through the years I addressed his issues one at a time and learned the best ways to reach him and teach him.

All of our children are unique although they may share many similar traits. Once we know how their minds work, what their abilities, areas of interests and strengths are, we have a much better chance of guiding them towards independence.

However, what truly surprised me was when Brandon was able to overcome many of his weaknesses. That was when his development began to soar. I believe he surrendered to them just as the following quote from Dr. Moshe Feldenkrais suggests: *Find your true weakness and surrender to it. Therein lies the path to genius.* I am not implying that my son is a genius but he continues to surprise me when it comes to his ongoing growth and development.

Your children will show you the way.

Who Is Doing the Transitioning and To What Are You Transitioning?

Who is doing the transitioning, the child or the parents? Ideally, along the way we would all be transitioning together as a family. We must have a plan, a destination, and know what our goals are.

How can you help your child grow and change if you are not growing and changing yourself?

As you raise your child you must be the best you can be. You lead the way and you hold the key to your child's future. As you continue to grow and change you become a more evolved human being in the process.

Find ways to take time out for yourself, and bring laughter and joy into your life. As parents, you set the tone within the family unit. The healthier you are emotionally and physically the better you will feel, and you will be more available and present for your child and those around you.

I used to say the better you take care of yourself the more you will have to give, especially to those you love. I recently added that the better you take care of yourself the longer you will live. Of course, there is no guarantee, but as a mother I make conscious choices every day to help extend and improve the quality of my life.

As I have said before, you must get help and support from people who care and understand your child. You do not need to do this alone. There are people out there who truly want to help. Welcome them in and allow them to assist and support you. When you parent this way, you and your entire family will benefit greatly.

Independence Will Look Different for Each Child

Your child is continually growing and changing. You may not be aware of it or even notice it unless you stay focused on the "small" actions and accomplishments in your child's life. For Brandon's thirty-sixth birthday, I took him out for lunch to his favorite restaurant. I could hardly believe my eyes when he walked over to the soda fountain to fill his glass with lemonade and put a plastic lid on the container. He easily peeled the paper off the straw and poked it into the hole on the lid. For years he had struggled unsuccessfully to master this simple task. Yes, tears rolled down my face as I watched him prep his glass and take a sip of his lemonade *just like everyone else*. He asked why I was crying. I told him it made me so happy to see him accomplish something he always wanted to do.

Many may see this as something small or they may not see it at all, but to me it was grand. Brandon had never before been able to manage this task on his own, although he wanted to so very badly. An acute lack of fine motor skills had always kept him from doing simple tasks like this one. But clearly he could do this now with great ease. With perseverance and much trial and error, he was able to finally accomplish it all on his own. Not only was this something to celebrate, but being able to master this task told me that he could achieve other things that he was not able to do before.

Again, that is why I continue to say that *by living life our children learn life*.

How I Found the Courage to "Let Go."

My ex-husband passed away at an early age and I became solely responsible for Brandon's wellbeing as an adult. It wasn't easy. Brandon seldom asked for anything while growing up, but at age twenty-three when he told me he wanted to live on his own, I was shocked.

Honestly, I never expected my son to live independently. All the while Brandon was growing up the professionals who worked with him repeatedly told us he would never be able to live alone. That message sunk in deeply. I was young and I put the professionals on a pedestal and I believed what they said. Now knowing how wrong they were is a very important message for me to pass on to you. *You do not have to automatically believe any negative comments made about your child, no matter who makes them.*

Brandon's request was so unexpected that I needed time and space to process it all. Just thinking about finding him an apartment and setting it up for him made me anxious and fearful. After much contemplation I made a deal with him. If he went back to the Vocational Independence Program (VIP) in New York (see Appendix) for his final year I would find him an apartment and we would try it out for six months and see how it went.

When the time comes for you and your child to physically separate and your child is on his/her own, you may walk around feeling lost or as if you have forgotten something. That feeling can become unnerving. This is normal and to be expected, due to the close bond you have established over the years. *However, I want to reassure you that over time it will lessen.*

For the first six months Brandon was on his own I never slept a wink. I was afraid for my son's safety every moment of every day. How would he monitor his time? What would he do? Where would he go? What would he eat? Would he sleep through the night? Would he hang out with the wrong people? I had hundreds of questions like these swirling around in my brain night after night, all night long. I was totally exhausted and stressed out, always questioning whether what I did was right.

During the daylight hours I would spend all my time with Brandon showing him around his new neighborhood and familiarizing him with the bus routes, local pharmacies, restaurants, grocery stores, and answering any questions he had about work or anything else. He had a job coach from Best Buddies who was helping him adapt to his new part-time job at a retail store. It was crucial having someone there he could talk to and who understood him, which helped him feel more at ease.

I wanted my son to succeed so I put all my attention toward helping him for those six months, as planned. I am very happy to say it paid off. At this writing Brandon is forty-one, and he continues to mature and move forward. Just yesterday he was able to express how he felt to someone other than me. It was a day for celebration. Though he has challenges to face each and every day, it is beautiful to be able to watch him learn from them and progress.

What continues to be most difficult is that no one has been able to stop Brandon from having seizures. These seizures continue to rip his life apart and have caused him to lose several jobs. Approximately 30% of people who have epilepsy are unable to have their seizures controlled by any type of medication. At this time, there are no answers. Along with medication Brandon goes for holistic treatments (the B.E.S.T. technique) and in many ways it is helping. His thinking is much clearer and his communication skills have also improved, but his seizures continue.

How my son is able to have a strong, positive attitude and move forward after falling down and frequently ending up in the hospital is absolutely amazing to me. This is another fabulous attribute he has and is another lesson for me to learn.

Are You Making Excuses For Your Child?

Many of the parents I work with continually make excuses for their special needs adult child. By doing this they avoid the issues that push their own personal hot buttons. They prefer to maintain the status quo and leave things just as they are.

Making excuses and allowing your adult child to slide as you look the other way is not a wise approach. You may think it makes you feel better and takes the immediate pressure off of you to make plans now, but it will not get you or your child anywhere.

> *Courage is not the absence of fear, but rather the judgment that something else is more important than fear.*
>
> Ambrose Redmoon

I am continually asked how I found the courage to allow my son to live independently. The above quote explains it well. I lived with fear constantly but I knew early on that it was more important to focus on Brandon's independence than on my fears. I realized that is how courage develops.

Start with a basic plan and develop it over time. Be realistic while being optimistic. It is crucial not to allow fear to overrule your vision and allow it to cloud your thoughts and decision making. If your decision making is based on fear, you are doing a disservice to your child and yourself.

Through Loving Eyes

The next time you look at your child try evaluating your son or daughter from your heart, through loving eyes. Make sure you take into consideration all the traits that do not exist on any standardized tests. You must look at your child from a very different perspective than the professionals do. You know your child best so when you look at your child from now on, see what it is that you like best about your son or daughter. I promise you there will be many attributes that will make you smile. Take them into consideration when you are planning for your child's future. Give special attention to those areas. They are sure to lead you in the right direction. Don't forget to monitor your fears, especially when you are around your child. Special needs kids are extremely sensitive and intuitive so do not allow your fears to become your child's fears.

Our child's life will never be perfect, not even if he or she is neurotypical. Every time the thought of independence for your child comes up, allow yourself to feel the negative emotions that arise; don't stuff them down, just feel them. You may have several emotions wrapped inside of fear. Fear and safety seem to be the most common of all, but often there are more underlying emotions beneath them. You will need to uncover those feelings and release them before you and your adult child can move forward.

Below are some key words that will most likely trigger some emotions. The exercise here is to find out why these emotions are being triggered and work on befriending them. Read the words below and note your initial reaction to them. How does each word make you feel? Name the emotions that arise. Commit to being open and honest with your emotions. After recognizing a feeling, talk to it. Yes, talk to it. I often ask, "What are you here to teach me?" In stillness and in time you are sure to get an answer.

- Believe
- Trust
- Surrender
- Give Up Control
- Let Go
- Be Flexible
- Be Willing
- Allow
- Be Open Hearted
- Be Open Minded
- Befriend Uncertainty

Write Down a List of Your Fears and the Pros and Cons for Each One

Revisit this page daily and see how you feel, and note whether any of your fears actually came true. Photocopy this page and continue to write down your fears every day and reread what you wrote the following day. Over time you will see that most of your fears never happened. This exercise will help to strengthen and build up your courage.

FEARS	PROS	CONS

1. _____

_____

2. _____

_____

3. _____

_____

4. _____

_____

5. _____

_____

6. _____

_____

7. _____

_____

8. _____

_____

9. _____

_____

10. _____

_____

The Future Is One Giant Question Mark

Is your adult child capable of some type of independence? How about starting out right where they are today? Begin by personalizing your child's room and making it more adult-like and "mature." Little by little, give your child responsibilities and privileges; observe how well your son or daughter handles them, and add more as they are mastered.

Another great alternative is a guesthouse, or a converted garage on the same property. If this is a possibility, it is an ideal way to teach your adult child to live alone, under your watchful eye. I talk more about this in Chapter Eight.

Families who have a special needs child often develop codependent relationships.

Yes, many parents dislike hearing the word "codependence" and I felt that way too for many years. There are times I feel the thread of codependency is still with me today. But it does not surprise me that codependency occurs because the time parents spend with a special needs child far exceeds the time spent with their other children. Most autistic children have few or no friends and will spend most of their time at home with their parents. Their siblings spend much more time away from the house, with their friends and involved in activities. It is just a fact. It is extremely difficult to wean a special needs adult child. Over the years, we become attached to each other like "glue."

Letting Go: Stuck Like Glue

If you were to combine super glue, wallpaper paste and fly paper you would end up with a concoction that would most likely stick forever. That is how it has felt for many of my clients and for me as well when the time came to begin to "let go." It is an extremely difficult time and often it feels nearly impossible to endure, especially in the beginning.

I know firsthand that it is not that you don't want to let go. It is that you have had the role of caregiver since your child was little and stepping back terrifies you. Not knowing what the future holds for your special needs child only compounds your fear, stress, and anxiety.

I have worked with many parents and *fear is the underlying emotion* which they all share in common. They all fear what will happen to their child if their child is given more "freedom." Yet, they want their child to become as independent as possible. *Trying to harmonize these opposing feelings is a constant battle.*

I understand that parents are overwhelmed by the lack of vocational, social, educational and living opportunities available for special needs children, and that their child's safety is their number one concern.

Letting go is not easy, but it must be done if you want your child to achieve independence. You are not going to live forever, so please, while you are here, help your child reach maximum independence. Then, when you are gone, your child will have the tools and experience that will make it easier for him/her to carry on. Allow your tears to flow and watch your negative emotions lift as you and your child cross over to independence—one day and one step at a time.

Teaching parents about the "letting go" process is crucial. Once they understand the process many of my clients have been able to loosen the reins and allow their children more freedom and space. It is not an easy transition for a child and is often as difficult for parents, if not more so.

We need to focus more on the parents.

Again, professionals focus all their time on the children with no time spent on the parents. How can adult children learn to be free and independent when the people in charge of their wellbeing, their parents, have little or no tools to help them make this transition? Without the tools or the means to actually see how it is done, most parents will remain trapped by their own fears—not because they want to be, but because they know no other way. This will paralyze any progress they could be making and can cause them to remain stuck in fear forever. *No matter how many unique housing facilities or communities we create around the globe the huge problem of independence will continue if parents are unable to "let go" in a timely and positive manner.*

Are You Overprotective?

It is tough to find a parent raising a child with autism and special needs who isn't overprotective. How could we be anything else? We see how very naïve our child is. We know that he/she is easy prey and a target for bullying. Our child acts and does things differently than other children, and inevitably stands out in a crowd.

It is an unwritten oath that moms and dads will protect their children at all costs. After our first glance of our newborn we automatically fly into protection mode. If and when we cannot protect them we feel as if we have failed. That is a hard pill to swallow. I know it well, too well. When Brandon was in elementary school he was often bullied, tormented, and teased. I tried to keep my son safe by volunteering at his school as often as I could, but even that did not help. Though this was more than thirty years ago, I can remember those deep sad feelings as if it were yesterday. Not only was I grief stricken for my son, I agonized over my inability to protect him at all times and keep him from getting hurt.

With that said, this is why most of us become overprotective. Add to that a lack of sleep, stress, anxiety, fear of the future, etc., and over time our bond to our special needs child can become superglued. When we are asked to step aside and allow our child to grow and possibly live outside the home most of us are unable to make that transition or adjustment, *even if our child can.*

One day you will no longer be here and if you have not done everything you can to help your child succeed then you have not kept your unwritten oath of keeping your child safe. If your child has little to no outside experiences how do you think your son or daughter will survive after you and your spouse are no longer around?

The good news is that if you are reading this you still have the opportunity to let go and allow your child to reach maximum independence. By doing this your child will have a much better chance of adapting after you are gone.

No One Knows How Your Child Will Cope With Losing You

I am often asked, "Do you know how much Brandon will miss you? You say he does not show much emotion and does not say much when it comes to feelings. How do you know how he will feel after you are gone?"

My answer is, I truly do not know how he will feel nor do I know how he will act. *What I do know is that he will need help.* I mention this because I believe *every parent should make a written plan, no matter what special needs their child has.*

The fact is you cannot predict how your child will react to your passing. Some special needs children will understand it and grieve appropriately, while others will not. Let me give you an example. When Brandon was twenty-three, he had to go through his father's funeral, his grandmother's passing, and his dog's death, all within a six-month period.

Let's begin with his dad's funeral. At the service in the chapel, Brandon laughed while we all cried. It made his older brother furious. People stared, puzzled and irritated by his strange reaction. It forced me to dig deep and to try to understand what was going on inside my son. I saw that Brandon was "tee-hee-hee-ing," which is his nervous laugh, the one he uses when he does not know what proper emotion to express. Trying to explain this to others who are grieving at a funeral is simply impossible to do.

When my mom passed away, who was Brandon's best friend, we talked about her. In this case, with his limited way of expressing his feelings, he was able to say he was going to miss her. And later, when his dog Archie died, this seemed to be the easiest loss for Brandon to show emotion. He seemed sad and he shed a few tears, which actually seemed forced. However, later that year, Brandon asked me for photos of his dad, grandmother, and dog. Seventeen years later he still has those photos displayed on a shelf in his apartment.

I don't know how Brandon will feel once I am gone, but I do know he will feel the loss and he will need people to help him, as I have all these years. I want him to continue on with his independent life that together we worked so hard to create.

No one knows how *anyone* will deal with the loss of a loved one. My mother died more than sixteen years ago and I still miss her dearly. However, as I go on I keep my mother's beautiful traits alive in my positive actions each and every day.

Let's hope that your child will move along with the beautiful traits that you leave behind. Let that be your goal as you build a strong network of people to help your child carry on.

I Lost My Footing

Just recently I completely lost my footing as fear knocked me over. Brandon again needed to change his seizure medications, and while the doctor was trying to get the correct dosage his seizures began to escalate. I know how difficult it can be switching from one medication to another. Even knowing this, it caught me off guard and I began to act overprotective.

I began worrying about Brandon's seizures and I called him incessantly to see how he was doing. He soon let me know that he didn't need or want me to do this. Yet, I was unable to stop this obsessive behavior, which truly surprised me. Fear grabbed hold of me when I least expected it. When I finally was able to step back and understand what was happening to me I was able to stop myself from calling, and I began to trust again, as I had learned to do over the years. *When the well-being of your adult child is at risk it is difficult to find that middle ground as a parent where you are not overbearing yet still loving and caring.* It takes practice, and as you can see, after forty-one years I am still learning.

As I have said, independence is like a dance. You need to know when to step in and when to step out. With that said, there are days when I could not find the beat and my musicality seemed to be off. I stepped in when I was supposed to step out. Even after all these years waves of fear can still catch me off guard and my overprotective tendencies will appear out of nowhere. When this happens, I have to reevaluate the way I am treating Brandon and to be aware that this old pattern in me still exits. However, once I become aware of what I am doing I am usually able to stop the behavior and work through the situation more quickly and gracefully.

Growing into independence is a lifelong process for you and your child. Be kind to yourself and keep moving forward one day at a time, just as you ask your child to do.

Bullying, Educating, and More Letting Go

Brandon has been bullied all his life, and he still is, even as an adult. Unfortunately, the bullying has not changed, but the way he handles himself has.

The more your children are exposed to the "real world" the more they learn. Yes, bad things do happen to good people, but without having firsthand experiences how else will your children learn? You do not have to have a disability to have bad things happen; they happen to everyone.

I often conduct workshops on bullying for special needs adult children. It might surprise you to learn that many of our special needs adults do not know that they have choices. For example, if they are being harassed they often have a choice to simply walk away. In one of my recent workshops a young man declared, "I never thought of that!" As I wrote in one of my teaching stories, my son said the same thing. We must educate our children about bullying just as we do with everything else. I talk more about this in Chapter Eight.

It is crucial that we do not stop our children from advancing because we are living in the future, in the "what if" zone where most of our fears never happen.

A Spiritual Teacher

By now most people have heard of Eckhart Tolle, the spiritual teacher and author of *The Power of Now,* and numerous other books. Tolle often talks about letting go of negative thoughts and attitudes and "living in the now." His teachings have helped me learn how to apply the process of letting go.

Tolle suggests visualizing yourself holding a hot coal in your hand. You have two choices. You can hold onto it or you can simply open your hand, release it and let it go. It sounds so simple and sometimes it is. However, in some situations it is much more complex and difficult, and sometimes we ourselves make it that way. How successfully our children are able to negotiate through life when we are gone will depend in part on our ability to let go now. Do start thinking about ways you can start this process. It may take some time so be patient with yourself as you continue to practice it daily. If you do nothing more at first than read the above paragraph over and over again, it will help you begin to embrace the concept. I found it a wonderful place to start.

Begin Within

When you walk to the edge of all the light you have and you take that first step into the darkness of the unknown, you must believe one of two things will happen. There will be something solid for you to stand upon or you will be taught how to fly.

Dr. Patrick Overton

I am a strong believer in hanging great quotes around my house that resonate with my being. The above quote helped me tremendously. I posted it in my living room to give me strength and courage. Over the past seventeen years Brandon and I have, in many ways, learned how to fly, and when we are not flying we always find something solid to stand upon. I am confident that this will happen for you and your child, too.

An Interesting Thought Struck Me on Thanksgiving Day

If I were an artist painting a picture, would I know when it was complete and time to stop before I went overboard and ruined it? I began to learn the answer to that question later on that day.

I spent several hours with Brandon before we headed over to our Thanksgiving feast. It was one of those rare days when we were both feeling out of sorts. I seemed to get in his way and he got in mine. After a few hours together I was exhausted and it appeared that he was, too.

Sad to say, these conditions prompted my overbearing mothering tendencies to come out in full force. I tried to rein myself in, but feeling out of sorts only added to my lack of self-control. Brandon was irritable and our personalities clashed, which is something that does not happen very often (for which I am grateful).

As we were coming out of his apartment, Alice, one of his neighbors, walked by and asked, "Brandon, is that your Mom?" He quickly replied, "Yes." Alice then said to me, "Your son is a very nice person and we talk often." In the past, when I have asked Brandon if he talks to anyone in his apartment complex, his answer has always been no. I am aware that he has a personal life that he keeps to himself, as we all do. He is an adult and has the right to his privacy. But this just confirmed to me he has more going on than meets the eye, and I was happy to have that information.

I often am able to get myself out of a negative situation and salvage something worthwhile from the experience, and in this instance I did just that.

As hard as this is to write I knew I needed to write it. Though I teach the art of "letting go" and have been walking on the independence path with my son for a very long time, I need to make sure I do not idealize our circumstances and to give an honest account of my life experiences with Brandon. My son does not need me any more in ways he used to, which is wonderful. The difficult part is stepping back from my son and allowing him the freedom to live his life on his own terms. Brandon is forty-one years old, he is considered a middle-aged man, and as you can see, letting go is still a challenge for me. *I write about this so you won't be surprised or discouraged when you are challenged, either by your child or by circumstances, to soldier through the many stages of letting go.* This is a very long process, which is good news because I believe that most of us are going to need time to properly achieve this goal.

If I were an artist I would consider my picture to be complete. I am able to step back and admire the painting that Brandon and I created together. I am going to continue to move back even further than I ever have before. I believe this new level of freedom will be the most loving gift I can give not only to Brandon, but to myself as well.

Summary

There have been many precepts that have helped me move along this path and helped my son accomplish his dream of independence. I would like to share some of them with you.

- Trust and believe in yourself and the decisions you make.

- Find something positive in every situation.

- Stay centered and balanced by eating well and taking good care of yourself.

- Find someone you trust with whom you can share your deepest feelings.

- Discover a way to vent frustration or any unwanted emotions. I found writing to be a great tool.

- Laughter is a necessity. Be silly. Rent a funny movie, laugh out loud, and enjoy the moment.

- Live in the now, the present moment.

- Be kind to yourself. Do something just for pleasure, even if only for a few minutes each day.

- Get all the care and help and support you can, as often as you can.

- Follow your heart and you will never get lost.

Surrender and "Let Go"

I hung the following piece, "Let Go," on my wall. It has been an excellent reminder of why "letting go" is so very important and how to achieve it. I read it often and it always gave me a lift. You might try hanging it on your wall for inspiration. It truly has helped me and I believe it could help you as well.

Let Go

Anonymous

"Let Go......"

To "let go" does not mean to stop caring,
It means I can't do it for someone else.

To "let go" is not to enable,
but to allow one to learn from natural consequences.

To "let go" is not to be in the middle arranging all the outcomes,
but to allow others to affect their own destinies.

To "let go" is not to nag, scold, or argue,
but to search out my own shortcomings and correct them.

To "let go" is not to adjust everything to my desires,
but to take each day as it comes, and cherish myself in it.

To "let go" is not to fix,
but to support.

To "let go" is not to regret the past,
but to grow and live for the future.

To "let go" is to fear less,
and to love more.

May every day be your Independence Day!

Notes

Eight

You Need to Have a Plan

Four steps to achievement: Plan purposefully. Prepare prayerfully. Proceed positively. Pursue persistently.

William A. Ward

You Need to Have a Plan

When your neurotypical children leave the nest many of you will have your special needs child as a permanent nester. You simply need to have a plan. A plan is not only necessary, it can also be comforting.

When I was a young gal and before I had children, I used to fly by the seat of my pants. Once I had my two sons, life took on a whole new meaning. Then when I found out I had a son with special needs my mental outlook and plans changed dramatically. I was silently asked to see life differently and to learn all I could to help him live the best life possible. It has been loads of hard work and I am not about to stop now. I know I need to make a plan and take action if I want my son to continue to live a successful independent life now and after I am gone.

Whenever we embark on new territory we will need a road map to find our way. Before your child reaches adulthood is when you will need to rely on your own personal map to set your plan in motion.

To get started, ask yourself these important questions on pages 130-137, 147, and make sure your answers are honest and realistic.

- Where is my child right now emotionally, physically and intellectually?

___

- What makes my child happy? What does he/she enjoy?

___

- What are my child's learning strengths, abilities and interests?

___

- What makes my child sad, angry and frustrated?

___

- In what areas does my child excel?

- Is my child able to make his or her own decisions?

You Need to Have a Plan

- Does my child have behavioral, safety and social needs?

___

- Can my child handle finances and pay the bills?

___

- Will my child be able to work?

- Can my child be left alone and unmonitored for long periods of time?

- Can my child function in society without me there all the time?

- What do I see for my child's future? How does it look to me and how does it look to my child? Do we see it the same way? Are our views different? This is an extremely important area to look at.

- What type of lifestyle do you each envision, including geographic preferences? For example: Does your child want to live with or close to a relative or a family friend? Do *you* want your child to live with or near a relative or friend? *It's important to make sure that you are asking these questions of yourself and your child. Wherever possible and within reason, your child's wishes need to be considered first.*

_____
_____
_____
_____
_____
_____
_____
_____
_____

Take Action
1. Frequently explore your child's strengths and interests; it will help to determine the direction you need to go.
2. Be flexible and open to change as you move along the path. Although we start down one path we often end up on another.
3. Be positive as you teach your child chores and assign responsibilities; the sooner the better.

How Does Your Child's Future Look Today?

Has anything changed? Do you have anything new to write about?

Every plan will look different. Of course, over time your plan will change. Start where you are today. Put it on your calendar to revisit these pages once a month and update them. This will help you identify the direction your child is moving. You may see twists and turns that your son or daughter may have taken, which will move you to possibly consider a new direction on the path. Even if you find that nothing has changed, this exercise will confirm that you are on track. It will help you find peace within yourself and ease your fears for your child's future.

- Plans for My Child's Future

_____
_____
_____
_____
_____
_____
_____
_____
_____
_____
_____
_____
_____
_____
_____
_____

I Have Autism...What'll I Do Without You, Mom?

Give Your Child Choices Along the Way

In many areas, children with special needs mature more slowly than neurotypical children. However, it is crucial to give them the space to grow as we encourage, support and love them along the way. Just as we would not always carry our walking toddlers around for fear they will fall down, we have to allow our adult children to fail, to learn from their own experiences and get back up all by themselves.

It is like building a fence around your adult child to create a safe haven. We know that is not possible, and if it were it would never work. What will work is to picture an imaginary fence around your child, with space to grow, and moving the imaginary fence further out each time you see progress. If you discover an area your child is unable to conquer you may need to find another way. For example, if your child cannot drive or use a bicycle, he/she will need to learn how to use public transportation or call for a taxi.

Also, we all will have some non-negotiables that our children must do and conditions that must be met. For me they were, and still are, that Brandon takes his medication every day, that he is not hurting anyone and no one is hurting him.

Where to Begin

Are you an enabler? Would you like to see your adult child make more progress?
Here are several suggestions:
1. If you have a tight grip, loosen it.
2. You need to be aware if you are in the "compression" or "expansion" stage. The compression stage is when you are worried or filled with fear and your thoughts and actions keep you and your child from moving forward. The expansion stage is when you are able to trust and let go of your fears. You can see the bigger picture and are able to stay on course and move ahead.
3. Be firm and consistent with your rules, but kind at the same time.
4. Stop hovering. Take several steps back and become an observer.
5. Allow your adult child the space to succeed and fail; it is a necessary combination for achieving independence. I say this often because most parents become fearful when they see their child fail, but it is part of the learning process.

6. Teach your adult child basic skills such as how to read a bus schedule, cooking, household chores, and anything else that you feel would be an essential skill for your child to have. Have *fun* doing it no matter how long it takes or how it turns out. The key word is *fun*. When you are able to add fun to your teaching moments it will make life much easier and more enjoyable for the entire family.

Teach From Your Heart First, Then From Your Head
Stop controlling and learn to live in the "not knowing."

- Praise your child often.

- Do not allow your adult child to consume your entire life. Those days are over. You must make sure to take time for yourself.

- Watch your demeanor and your verbal delivery. Routinely check your fears, frustrations and overall attitude.

- Think positive and chances are you will be positive.

Moving From Fear to Freedom and Independence

- Communicate appreciation to your child.

- Spur your child on and be sure your son or daughter knows you believe in them.

- Help your child learn to solve personal problems and navigate obstacles.

- Be a helpful guide.

- Encourage your child to learn to get things done on his/her own.

- Be broadminded.

I discovered that when I was able to help my son in a heartfelt, kind and gentle way it proved to be a more positive experience for both of us. I became aware of how *not* to intrude in his space and respect him for who he is. The following ways helped Brandon immensely. They are a "recap" of the principles I found to be the most effective.

- Guide, don't Force
- Instruct, don't Insist
- Demonstrate, don't Demand
- Suggest, don't Struggle
- Encourage, don't Pressure

As long as my son gets the job done it's *good enough* for me.

Walk your talk, be a good role model and offer your adult child choices and options along the way. Watch how your child matures when encouraged to learn through firsthand experiences.

Games to Accelerate Independence

Brandon, at age thirty-seven, still had a hard time clearly communicating his thoughts. He knew what he wanted to say, but most often it did not come out of his mouth the way he intended. Explaining himself and expressing his feelings always was, and still is, extremely difficult for him. He is often misunderstood. This makes my son an easy target, because he cannot protect and defend himself with words.

Today he is better at expressing himself and his feelings with me because he trusts me, but he still has difficulty communicating with everyone else. His low affect and inability to understand others often gets him into trouble in the social arena, which hurts him deeply.

I regularly help him in this area and I try to make it fun, not work. I have created games to help boost Brandon's self-esteem, confidence and verbal skills, giving him a better understanding of everyday life. Since I have implemented these games I have seen marked improvement in my son's demeanor, attitude and skills. He is now aware that we play these games to encourage growth in areas he struggles with.

I don't make up a game just because I wish my son would do better in a particular area. I create these games when Brandon voices that he does not understand how to do something or cannot do something and wishes he could.

I hope that one day he will be able to master all the areas he wants to conquer and talk to others the same way he talks to me, so that when he is out in the world people will finally get a glimpse of what a sweet, kind, intelligent man he truly is.

I love games; they set an upbeat tone and create a positive teaching mode that makes lessons easier to digest. The following examples of "games" I have created can be used with anyone at any age. I still use them with Brandon.

Eating By Color

All the food on Brandon's plate used to be gray, beige or white. Several years ago I took him to his favorite restaurant, which features a huge glass case filled with food. I asked him to select three different dishes, two with a bright color and only one white, gray or brown. He selected carrots, green beans, and a piece of chicken. After he ate his meal he said how much better he felt. Making it fun while guiding him and giving him options made all the difference. He has been making better food choices ever since.

Repeating Himself

When Brandon gets stuck repeating himself I tell him in a soothing voice that he has twenty more times to say it and then we need to move on to something else. When the twentieth time comes around he usually has had enough and is willing to stop and move on. If he goes back to repeating himself I gently remind him that he's gone over the limit, which usually causes him to stop and sometimes even chuckle.

Thank You, You're Welcome, Please

It is not often my son says "thank you", "your welcome" or "please", although I have certainly tried to teach him. Now I just gaze at him when those words would be appropriate. I do not need to say anything. The look on my face indicates that I'm waiting for him to say something. He usually realizes he needs to fill in the blank and will offer the proper response, often accompanied by a lopsided grin.

Understanding Emotions and Feelings

Brandon cannot tell when someone is happy, sad, irritated or angry. Most emotions throw my son for a loop, which makes socializing nearly impossible. If you could only see me when I'm teaching Brandon how to interpret the facial expressions of others (I probably should create and post a video of it as it is rather entertaining). This game seems to work best in a public place such as a restaurant. I try to make sure he does not feel that we're "working," that he's just out having another meal with his silly Mom.

I sit across from Brandon, plaster an exaggerated smile on my face, and ask him, "How do you think I feel right now?" He usually laughs first and then tells me that I'm weird, funny, or bizarre. I explain in a kind voice that a smile usually means happiness, and is a "friendly" expression. Then I make an angry face. It makes him uncomfortable, but he gets that one more easily. We go through two or three facial expressions at a time, which seems to be quite enough. We both usually end up making fun of my weird faces. However, the job gets done and our goal is accomplished. I play this game with him a few times a year as a "refresher course."

I always make sure my son is in a receptive mood before I begin to teach him. If he is not I try again another time, when he is.

Your Child Will Want Some Freedom

Many people are surprised to hear that adult children with special needs want to be free to be themselves and to be independent. There are varying degrees of freedom and independence. Why shouldn't our children want to do what they can for themselves and be accepted and included as part of society? Freedom and independence are two of the greatest gifts we can give our children, whether or not they have special needs.

Independent Living Skills

Below is a list of important independent living skills that you may want to focus on right away or sometime in the future, depending on the age of your child.

- Grocery Shopping, Cooking, and Nutrition
- Budgeting and Check Writing
- Safety Skills and Anti-Bullying Techniques
- Laundry and Basic Housekeeping
- Social and Communication Skills for use in the "real world"

Your child may have difficulty in many of these areas, as did my son. To my amazement Brandon has been able to conquer most of these skills with everyday practice. The way Brandon went about it was often rather eccentric, but that's not what's important. My job was to let go of perfectionism and to deem Brandon's "creative" but adequate ways of doing things "good enough." Whenever a challenging task gets done I celebrate my son and his ability to accomplish goals that years ago were impossible for him to achieve. The more Brandon can do on his own the better for him now and when I am gone.

Safety

You cannot be careless or reckless when it comes to your child's safety. However, you cannot let your own paralyzing fears for your child's safety stop you from allowing your child to grow and go and live outside the family home, even if it scares you.

- No risk, no gain.
- Your fears are often an illusion.
- Many of us are worried and frightened of the unknown.
- Replacing the word *worry* with *wonder* is a more positive way to look at life. Worry is a negative emotion and uses a tremendous amount of energy, whereas Wonder is a brighter way of looking at the future and allows you to be more positive and hopeful.
- Our chattering and overthinking mind is often our worst enemy.
- We all learn life by living life.
- To ultimately be successful one may need to fail over and over again.
- Be aware of your fears and negative thoughts. Do not allow them to become your child's.

No Risk, No Gain

Encourage positive development throughout your child's lifetime. Do not rob your son or daughter of the everyday experiences that will encourage growth and the development of important new skills. As with anyone, this is a lifelong process. *Without firsthand personal experiences independence for a child with special needs will come late or not at all.*

Our adult children will learn best through trial and error and their own personal experience. We need to support and encourage and allow them to try new things, no matter how fearful or uncomfortable it makes us feel.

If our children fail, as my son has done, they will learn to get up, move on, and conquer yet another skill. Always keep in mind that the way a task is accomplished does not matter. Though it may take time and much repetition, stay focused on the process, not merely on the end result. Brandon has taught me that if given the opportunity to succeed, in most cases he will. If we concentrate on our children's willingness to move forward, and praise every achievement, no matter how small, it will encourage them to keep on trying.

Remember, no risk, no gain. Of course, we have to be smart about this; there is a big difference between encouraging our children to work on new and challenging skills in which there is the "risk" of temporary "failure," and allowing them to attempt something unwise or potentially harmful.

Stepping Stones

There are all levels of independence.

A study for Easter Seals (see Appendix) found that more than 80% of autistic adults between the ages of 19 and 30 were still living at home with their families.

If your child lives at home with you, periodically assess your son or daughter's room and do what you can to "mature" the décor as each new stage of development is achieved. Encourage your child to be part of this activity and to get involved in the process. Don't let your child get "stuck" in a self-concept that does not support growth and change. Assign household responsibilities that he or she can handle and when sufficiently mastered, add more. The key word here is "more," which will give your child opportunities to grow and perhaps one day live outside the family home.

If you are lucky enough to have a guest house on your property, an over-the-garage apartment or any space that you can convert into a small efficiency apartment, you will have the ideal circumstance for "independence training." If this is the case, I strongly recommend that you consider allowing your son or daughter to try to learn to live there "alone." Of course, if your child is fearful and does want to go it alone then I would recommend you have a family member stay with him/her initially. When your son or daughter feels more comfortable with the new arrangements he/she will be able to try it alone. Most of the adult children I have worked with have been able to move through this stage rather quickly. However, if your child shows no signs of interest at all you may want to introduce the idea periodically until interest is shown. I believe over time your child will see this as a good opportunity and eventually enjoy his/her new-found independence.

This is a wonderful option that would allow you to personally gauge and guide your child's progress from a close but nonintrusive distance.

Some special needs children and adults may live in an assisted living or group home, or on a specialized ranch or farm. When the time comes, one such arrangement may be the best housing option for your child. Some other options include:

1. Remaining at home on one's own with support and/or supervision
2. Living with relatives or friends
3. Renting an apartment or a home
4. Shared housing
5. Intentional communities
6. Licensed facilities
7. Transitional models
8. Supported living programs
9. Supervised living
10. Group homes in the community
11. Supervised agriculture and community farmsteads
12. Low income housing
13. Create your own There are families who are purchasing homes in communities that their children are familiar with. They are converting them into shared living spaces for their children to live in with round-the-clock supervision on the premises. For many this has worked out well. As parents it will help to think outside the box as your adult child becomes independent. You must be creative and find the ways that work best for your child.

The goal must be to find affordable, appropriate and secure housing to ensure that your child is not turned away or left to live in an undesirable circumstance.

What are Your Child's Needs?

Circle the ones that concern you and write about them below.
1. My child's behavior issues
2. Safety concerns
3. Social interactions
4. Will my child need supervision?
5. Can my child learn enough to live independently?
6. All the above
7. Add any additional concerns you may have

_____
_____
_____
_____
_____
_____
_____
_____
_____
_____
_____
_____
_____
_____
_____
_____
_____

I Have Autism...What'll I Do Without You, Mom?

Below are skills your child will need to learn in order to live independently. However, do keep in mind that these skills will be learned over time at your child's individual pace and will depend on your child's abilities. Many of us forget that achieving independence is a process that takes place one day at a time. It is important to know what type of support your son or daughter will need from day one. Before your child leaves home you must have your support services in place.

Personal: Learning Independent Living Skills

1. Marketing and Shopping
   How and where to buy healthy food, i.e., fruit instead of junk food, etc.

2. Meal Planning
   How to prepare simple, easy, nutritious meals

3. Housecleaning and Laundry
   How and when to do chores

4. Budgeting and Banking
   How to pay bills on time and manage a checkbook

5. Public Transportation
   Learning the bus, train and subway routes, fares, and schedules

6. Healthcare, Hygiene and Safety
   A) Making doctor appointments, managing medication, insurance management
   B) How to take care of hygiene and personal grooming
   C) How to stay safe by knowing the neighborhood and surrounding areas; knowing when and how to make appropriate choices, such as simply walking away from a gang or knowing where it is unsafe to go.

<u>Household Inventory—The Bare Essentials</u>
Household Items
   A. Food: Staples such as bread, cereal, milk, peanut butter and jelly, etc.
   B. Drinking water
   C. Canned goods, etc.

      D. Paper goods
      E. Kitchen Items: Dishes, glassware, pots, pans, silverware, utensils
      F. Office Supplies: Stamps, envelopes, scissor, tape, pens, pencils, etc.
      G. Cleaning supplies: Soaps, cleanser, mop, broom, vacuum, laundry detergent, etc.

Toiletries
      A. Toothbrush, toothpaste
      B. Soap, shampoo, gel, hairbrush, comb
      C. Deodorant, hand and body lotion
      D. Band-Aids
      E. Feminine products
      F. Electric shaver

Emergency Gear
      A. Flashlight and batteries
      B. Extra two-week supply of medication
      C. Extra drinking water
      D. Emergency phone numbers
      E. Reserve of canned goods, granola bars, nuts, etc.
      F. Cell phone

<u>Community</u>
Relating to Others By:
1. Gaining socialization skills
2. Improving communication skills
3. Interacting appropriately with others
4. Making appropriate choices and decisions
5. Learning how to manage time
6. Learning how to relieve stress
7. Learning how to make/keep friends
8. Getting acquainted and familiar with their community

Vocational Skills in the Workplace
1. Finding ways to communicate clearly with co-workers and employers
2. Learning how to act and interact appropriately while at work

3. Learning techniques to manage various stress levels
4. Being able to ask for help and support when needed
5. Being included with co-workers if and when they desire

Do keep in mind that the above lists will take time for your child to master, as it is a process. The areas that come easy to your child will be mastered first, with the more challenging skills acquired progressively over the years. As I have mentioned before, though Brandon has been living independently for seventeen years, he has not achieved half of the items on the lists, yet he is still a success story.

The Workplace

Match the job choice to what your child enjoys doing and excels in. It can be a winning combination, as they most often work together.

As parents, you must advocate for the best possible vocational placement for your child. A study by the Easter Seals foundation revealed that 80% percent of adults on the autism spectrum are unemployed or underemployed and have trouble holding steady jobs. It is not that they are unable to perform their work tasks, because most often they can. However, they tend to have difficulty with socializing, communicating, and are often unable to interact appropriately with others in the workplace. These limitations cause many autistic adults to lose their jobs.

I learned firsthand how essential it is to have a job coach or mentor from the very first day on the job. If it were not for Brandon's job coach he would not have lasted very long at any of his jobs. His coach's assistance was invaluable. However, having a job coach did not stop him from having seizures. His seizure activity would escalate while at work due to on-the-job stress. He has been let go from several jobs because of this. The employers did not want to take on the responsibility and liability of him getting badly hurt while at work. Brandon took this very personally. He felt he was not good enough, and he would tell people that he was fired, which was not the case. Brandon's self-esteem plummeted and it has taken years to rebuild his confidence. *When our kids fall, they fall hard, and it often takes a very long time to bring them back.*

What does Brandon do for work now?

One of the questions I am frequently asked is, "What does your son do for work?" When I reply that he does not work right now because his seizures have escalated, people initially seem disappointed. But quite honestly my son does "work." In fact, he works harder than most people I know. He sets up his doctors' appointments and he shows up on time. He orders his medications and he never runs out. He shops at the grocery store and prepares his own simple meals. He does his own laundry and schedules a woman to come in every three weeks to clean his apartment. He excels in numbers so his checkbook is always balanced and up to date. *He basically takes care of himself by himself. This is a huge accomplishment.* So he does work hard every day to maintain his independent lifestyle, which he loves.

Once Brandon's seizures are under control he will return to work. However, he will be looking for a job that better suits him, one with minimal stress. In the meantime, he has created his own job of sorts, which is helping vendors who sell items from their carts on the outdoor mall near his house. He watches their carts when they take breaks and gets them food when needed. He likes doing it because he can show up when he feels well and if he is under the weather he doesn't have to go. He also likes the extra bit of cash he gets. It makes him feel good. This is exactly what he needs right now as he works on rebuilding his self-esteem and finding ways to reduce his seizures. I hope that in the future he will have a job that he is suited for and that suits him. He has been asked to accompany me and give a presentation at a few of my upcoming speaking engagements. Years ago, Brandon was a speaker for Best Buddies, which he really enjoyed. We will be trying it out locally to see how it goes.

Teaching Employees

My son once worked for a major corporation whose policy it was to hire a certain percentage of people with disabilities each year. I was asked to educate their employees on how to be more sensitive and understanding when working with people who have special needs. Overall, the program helped immensely.

However, there are people who cannot resist picking on others. This occurred while Brandon was employed, and, thankfully, the management did not stand for it. The young man in question was immediately put on probation and was told that if another incident occurred he would be fired. He knew they meant business and he straightened right up.

I have also had the opportunity to work with many autistic adults in the workplace. This is what I learned:

- Don't keep secrets.
- Allow people to know that your child has special needs.
- You must match your child's likes to what he or she can do well.
- Co-workers need to be educated and know what is expected of them.

Always treat your fellow workers the way you would like to be treated.

Be:
- Kind
- Understanding
- Respectful
- Forgiving
- Accepting of others

We need to continue to educate those who will be working with our sons and daughters and explain why our children do things differently and what they can do to help.

Being informed and having support from the management and employees will give our adult children a greater chance of making it in the workforce. Without it, most of them will not succeed. However, information is powerful and with proper education there is hope.

How to Gain Access to Services

As parents we want our concerns to be taken seriously, and to know that people genuinely care about us and our children. We would like to be treated kindly and have the professionals know that we want to be cooperative, but that sometimes we are simply overwhelmed and find ourselves at the end of our rope. We often are not at our best when trying to negotiate "the system," and we may find ourselves taking out our frustrations on the very people we are appealing to for help. We are trying our best to cope with the profound feelings of loss, sorrow, anger, irritation, resentment and disappointment that accompany the life of a parent with a special needs child. Most of us are chronically exhausted. We do not get weekends off, or any day off for that matter. We do not have adequate time to refuel or re-energize. We don't want to hear how bad our kid is doing and we don't want to add any additional work or stress to our already overwrought schedule. We can hardly manage what we have on our plate now. We obsess over our fears and find ourselves worrying constantly about the future.

Many of us have other children, and the demands of running even a "typical" household these days are challenging enough. But when you add a special needs child into the mix, it often becomes too much to bear.

I have a client who has a teenage daughter who has autism and learning disabilities. Her approach to teachers and counselors is to bully and threaten them in order to make them do what she wants. She is loud, pushy, and often obnoxious. She admits to being that way because she says it "works."

I told her that, yes, it might on the surface look as if it's working for you now but trust me, it's not working at all. No one likes to be treated that way, and sooner or later there will be a backlash. She said she didn't care as long as she was getting what she wanted for her daughter. I asked her, "But what kind of example are you showing her? These professionals may do what you say for now but if you continue to irritate and bully everyone it's going to backfire on you and your daughter, and before you know it you will be much worse off than when you began."

How do I know this so well? I was just like my client when my son was young. I attended meetings with a chip on my shoulder. I was tired, rude, easily irritated, and walked in the door angry. Then one day I realized that the people in the meetings were taking their cues from me, *not from my kind, gentle son*. That changed everything. I knew I had to act differently in order to get services for him, and I did.

I made it into a game. As you know by now, I love games; they're magical and they helped me get through the day.

I was determined to leave all of my negative feelings in an imaginary bag outside the door before entering the meeting room. I told myself that I could pick up the bag after the meeting was over and take it home. I soon discovered that I never wanted to pick it back up because I saw the positive results I was getting by being considerate and cooperative. That did not mean that I was timid and let myself be railroaded, or that I always agreed, not at all. My new approach was to be calm, cooperative and respectful. In other words, to treat the people in these meetings exactly the way I wanted them to treat me. I began to stand out from the other moms and dads and I began to receive services that other parents were not getting. It was working. After these meetings ended I felt empowered and so much better about myself because I no longer spoke in anger or was antagonistic and therefore did not leave these meeting embarrassed or chagrined. I had rediscovered my better self. Best of all, I got the results I wanted.

From that day forward I adopted a more positive outlook and pleasant demeanor. I knew that I was going to be on this road for a very long time and I was in favor of doing whatever I could to make it smoother and easier to navigate. This positive approach continues to work for me today. *I suggest you give this approach a try (I would love to hear how it worked for you).*

With services being almost non-existent in so many areas, especially for our adult children, we cannot afford to miss any opportunity to gain access to them.

Eligibility Varies From State to State

At age twenty-one your son or daughter will move from service entitlement to service eligibility and you will be the responsible party when you try to obtain services for your child later on.

How To Begin the Process
- Start early and include a transition plan in your child's Individualized Education Program (IEP).
- Be sure to include transition goals.
- If action on transition planning is taken early, it may extend your child's eligibility for support services when the school years end.
- You must stay on top of your child's progress and make sure that the necessary services for your child are being provided each step of the way.

Transition Services

Transition services are intended to prepare students to move from the world of school to the world of adulthood. Transition planning begins during high school at the latest. IDEA requires that transition planning start by the time the student reaches 16. It may start earlier than 16 if the IEP team decides it would be appropriate to do so. For more information, visit www.NICHCY.org.

Living Options

The Fish Story (A somewhat simple resolve)

I worked with a family who had a twenty-three year old autistic son, Brian. He was high functioning in many areas and wanted to live on his own. After a few sessions with the parents and the young man I discovered what was keeping the parents from letting him go. Brian was always losing his keys. The parents felt that if he lived alone and kept losing his keys they would have to be on call 24/7 to help him find them and let him into his house. If he could not reach them or if they were unavailable they feared he would panic and not know what to do. I asked the parents that if I could figure out a way to prevent Brian from losing his keys would they consider allowing him to live on his own. They both said yes.

While working with Brian I discovered that he loved all types of fish and mammals; in fact, his knowledge about them was encyclopedic. This gave me an idea. I took him to an art and hardware store for supplies and together we created a wall plaque using his favorite picture of a shark. He put hooks on the plaque and added a small wooden shark to his keychain. Though I helped a bit, he really made most of the plaque himself, which made it even more special and important to him.

Then we created a game. I explained that since the shark on his keychain matched the shark on the wall plaque, every time he walked into his house he was to hang his keys on the plaque before he did anything else. The wooden shark was so important to him that he took extra care to hang onto his keys while he was out.

It has been almost two years since he made that plaque and Brian has never lost his keys again. This story shows how important it is to know what captivates your child and to find a way to incorporate these interests creatively and meaningfully into your son or daughter's everyday life. A simple wall plaque with a picture of a shark with hooks and a matching keychain gave this young man freedom and independence that he otherwise would have been denied.

What About Our Severely Autistic Children?

Children who are severely autistic tend to get lost in the system. Many have been placed in institutions that are inappropriate. For now, there are very few truly adequate facilities where these children can live when their parents are unable to take care of them. I find parents can barely deal with this issue, and rightly so. It is daunting and discouraging, to say the least. However, if we continue to avoid the issue and just accept "what is" we will never be able to come up with better options and solutions. In order to change this we have to start talking about it now.

As a start, I have begun teaching a special training series for staff who work at these facilities. Parents have lamented to me that many of these institutions are understaffed, the employees undereducated, overworked, and underpaid. Over the years I also experienced this first hand. Even if the staff has sufficient knowledge to care for severely autistic children, they often are unkind, impatient and lack common sense. I am not sure why they have not been educated to know that a child who does not speak or show emotion still has the same feelings as everyone else. Autistic children are extremely sensitive and their feelings run deep. They deserve to be treated with kindness, respect and compassion, just as we all do.

Solutions can only be achieved if and when we talk openly about our concerns and follow up by taking action. *This is why, when the time comes, the Final Instructional Care Manual will be a crucial "tool of understanding" to help your child's networkers, caregivers, and service personnel provide the best care possible.*

If you will be looking for supported living for your child in the future, it is important to get your plan into your child's Individual Program Plan (IPP), so that a Regional Center can assist with the funding and help provide vendors. In California we have twenty-one Regional Centers. I have found them to be extremely helpful. In other states you will find the equivalent listed under Developmental Disability Services. Give them a call; you have nothing to lose and everything to gain.

Summary:
Positive Reinforcement Works
Having a positive attitude can work wonders.

I know how important a positive attitude is for all children, especially children with special needs. When I give Brandon positive feedback, compliments or praise his entire demeanor changes instantly and dramatically. He soaks it up like a sponge. I can see with my own eyes how it brightens him up. It's as if a ray of sunshine has lit up his world. The more positive input I give him the more he grows and develops. It is as if I am giving him permission to be himself and to do his best.

In other words, I accept my son for exactly who he is, and he can feel it. We all want to feel acknowledged and appreciated for who we are.

If you want to see how your child responds to positive input, just give it a try.

What You Can Do to Expedite Your Adult Child's Independence
1. Stay focused on the positive.
2. Offer few basic choices.
3. Be flexible.
4. Encourage your child to get involved especially when he/she shows interest.
5. Quickly apologize when you have done something wrong and own up to it.
6. Listen kindly to what your child has to say.
7. Celebrate your child's uniqueness and differences.
8. Support your child with love and encouragement along the way.

When you are able to gain control over your own emotions you will find life will move more smoothly and easily for you and your entire family.

Change isn't easy, but it is the willingness to change that facilitates our growth, keeps us resilient, and helps us to evolve.

Anonymous

SECTION FIVE

Legal Matters
They Truly Do Matter

Nine

Financial Planning and Legal Matters

Wills, Guardianship and Much More

*Planning is bringing the future into the present
so that you can do something about it now.*

Alan Lakein

Putting this chapter together has been extremely difficult for me. I don't know about you, but I become comatose just thinking about finances and numbers. I found myself avoiding, even resisting, the prospect of preparing a financial plan for my son. Trying to understand, much less create a plan and attend to all the complicated legal matters that go with it made me want to jump into bed and pull the covers over my head. This took me by surprise as I am always the gal who is prepared and I rarely find myself procrastinating. I like to get things done ASAP.

It's not easy admitting that I was being irresponsible but to move forward I have to own up to it and start anew. After reading the following story you will better understand why I temporarily could not handle this critical task.

Where Did All the Money Go?
My husband, Rick, and I never properly secured the funds that we had saved for Brandon while he was growing up. Let me share what happened to us. Hopefully it will spare you from making the costly mistakes we did.

After twenty-two years of marriage I filed for a divorce. Rick could not accept that he had a son with a disability, despite years of witnessing Brandon's tonic-clonic seizures. His denial was rock solid, and consequently coping with Brandon's epileptic seizures was left entirely to me. Rick remarried soon after our divorce, and within three years he passed away. All along I believed nothing could happen to the account we had set up together for our son when he was nine years old. This account was created so we would both have to sign before any money could be disbursed. When one of us died the other person would have full control over the account.

After Rick passed away I had to go the bank to take his name off the account and put the account solely in my name. I was shocked when the banker told me that the account had been closed.

What I did not know was that the account was written with an *"either/or"* signatory clause rather than *"and,"* which would have required both our signatures. At the time we set up the account, I thought we had specified the latter. You can see how essential it is to pay close attention to terminology and to always read and reread all legal documents carefully before they are finalized and signed. Who would have thought how costly the words *and* or *either/or* could end up being. Yet those small words were huge and turned out to be the difference between securing Brandon's financial future or leaving him without a penny to his name.

Be sure to hire someone who knows what they are doing in the financial department. I advise you not to leave these matters in your family's hands; find a competent neutral third party to handle it all. It is crucial that you engage an attorney or advisor who has a stellar reputation and a reliable track record. Do your homework and don't "settle" for just anyone; wait until you find the right person.

Richard, an old friend of mine, has been an attorney specializing in trusts for more than thirty years. When I asked him if he would help me with a Special Needs Trust for Brandon he quickly recommended that I find an attorney who specialized in them. Richard used to prepare them but over the years they changed so much and so often that he couldn't keep up and stopped offering that service.

When speaking at conferences and talking with my clients, I found that most parents are intimidated and overwhelmed by legal matters and the complexities involved in financial planning. It is not uncommon for them to procrastinate, as I did.

Financial Planning and Legal Matters...

This informational chapter was written to provide you with options on how to financially secure your special needs child's future. You will learn about different types of guardianships, trusts, wills, and more. Read the chapter carefully and see what approach best suits you and your family's needs.

I hope this information will eliminate some stress and make it easier for you to familiarize yourself with the legal terminology and the various options that are available. My goal is to motivate you to get your child's financial and legal house in order.

In this chapter you will find input from a well-known Attorney, a Certified Financial Planner, and a Certified Special Needs Planner.

As you make your way through this chapter be sure you listen to your instincts; don't go down any road that doesn't feel right to you. Visit the recommended sites and look around. If you wish, call and talk directly with someone. Do your homework and educate yourself on all the options before deciding which route or routes you are going to take.

I would like to begin by introducing you to Christopher A. Poulos, an attorney whose legal services focus on the rights of persons with developmental disabilities and their families. What makes him stand out from the crowd is that he is kind, generous, and extremely knowledgeable. He knows first-hand how difficult planning for the future can be for parents of special needs children because he, too, has an adult son with special needs. Despite a hectic schedule, he was very gracious and answered all of the following questions that were asked by my clients, patiently and thoroughly and in laymen's language, so the information would be easy to grasp.

LEGAL QUESTIONS AND ANSWERS

Q: What do I need to do legally to protect my autistic adult child?
A: Everything you need to do involves planning. Each child with autism is different and has different needs, different abilities and different disabilities. Based on your child's needs, you should make a plan of where you want your child to reside, what type of care or support your child will need in order to reside there, who should be the one in charge of your child's care and how much

your child's needs will require financially. Putting together a supported living plan takes forethought and no one knows better than you what circumstances are going to be best for furthering your child's growth and independence.

Simply having a plan is not enough to make the plan come to fruition. Your players must know your desires and put your game plan into effect. That is where an attorney's assistance comes into play. By obtaining a conservatorship or doing a Nomination of Conservators for your child, you are giving your successor the legal power to make decisions on behalf of your child. Setting up a Special Needs Trust to handle the financial burden of your child's care after you are gone, while allowing him or her to remain on government benefits, assists your successors in paying for your child's needs and ensuring that your child maintains the quality of life you desire. Funding the Special Needs Trust with enough money to pay for the plan for the remainder of your child's lifetime is also an important step. The Special Needs Trust cannot work if it is not adequately funded.

Q: What is a Letter of Intent? Will I need one?
A: A Letter of Intent is a way for you to communicate with your successors after you have passed away. The person or people taking over your child's care are probably not going to know all of your child's nuances the way that you do. The Letter of Intent is a way for you to tell them what type of care you want to see provided for your child and a way to tell them about your child's history. For example, some children have had surgeries or have allergies that should be noted or need a particular stuffed animal to fall asleep. You have spent your child's lifetime learning everything there is to know about caring for him or her, so a Letter of Intent is a way to avoid the need for your successor to "reinvent the wheel." They can pick up where you left off, making the transition from your passing as easy as possible on your child. The Letter of Intent is not a legal document and is not required in order for you to complete your planning; however, I typically recommend it to my clients as a tool to assist their successors. It can be updated or changed as often as you want.

Q: Will I need a Power of Attorney? I was told they are very easy to get. I was also told there are several different types.
A: A Power of Attorney is a document in which one person assigns authority to another person. There are as many different kinds of Powers of Attorney as there are types of authority you may need, such as financial, medical, educational or advocacy.

The catch with a Power of Attorney is if the signer does not have the requisite legal capacity, then the Power of Attorney is not valid. If your child signs a Power of Attorney for Health Care Decisions, naming you as the agent, a doctor could refuse to accept the Power of Attorney based on the fact that your child never had the capacity to sign it. A Power of Attorney can be useful if your child is high functioning and understands the document or if you want to give someone else authority on your behalf in the event that you are incapacitated.

If your child is unable to understand the Power of Attorney, a better alternative is a Conservatorship. A Conservatorship can give you the authority of multiple Powers of Attorney (access to records, educational, health, financial) plus additional authority (housing, social contacts, contracts). Additionally, the Conservatorship is done through Court Order and cannot be rejected by the person to whom it is presented.

The Financial Power of Attorney is a dangerous document as they are the most abused document in Financial Elder Abuse cases. A Financial Power of Attorney should be used with an abundance of caution and may not be necessary if your assets are in a living trust.

Q: How can I protect my child's assets and the money paid to him by the government if he is left money by friends and family members after I'm gone?
A: If your child is left money by a friend or relative at any time, it can be devastating to his or her government benefits. One way to avoid this is to tell anyone who may want to leave your child a gift, to leave it instead to the Special Needs Trust you have established.

In the event that someone does leave your child money directly, there are a few options to help get your child eligible for benefits again, based on the amount of money that was left to him or her. If the amount is minimal, your child's Conservator, agent or caregiver at the time can spend down the money to less than $2,000. They will want to do this within one month so that your child only loses one month of benefits.

If it is more than what can be spent down in one month's time, your child's agent, conservator, or caregiver can invest the money in exempt assets. Currently these include a burial plot, one vehicle, or the home where your child resides. If the gift to your child is substantial, a D-4 Special Needs Trust or a Court Ordered Special Needs Trust (in California) may be the only way to get your child back on government benefits.

Both of these types of Trusts will have government payback after your child is deceased. The right one to use will be based on the circumstances at the time and the state where you reside. The best way to handle this is to find an attorney who specializes in this area to assist your child's conservator, agent or caregiver.

Q: Do I need to name a guardian or trustee for my child? If I do not will the court appoint someone? What are the different types of guardianships and conservatorships? How do I decide which one would be best for my child?
A: It is not mandated that you name a Guardian or Conservator for your child; however, if you do nominate someone, the court puts a preference on the person you nominated to serve as guardian or conservator. The court does not typically appoint a guardian or conservator if there is no Petition (someone asking to serve in this role) before the court; however in some situations, the court may become aware that your child does not have a Guardian or Conservator and then will become involved. An attorney would be appointed by the court to find a suitable guardian or conservator (typically a family member). If one cannot be found, the court can appoint the Public Guardian or a Professional Conservator.

There are two types of Probate Conservatorships in the State of California. The first is a Limited Conservatorship. It is specifically designed for people with developmental disabilities and is most commonly used for persons who are Regional Center clients. In this type of Conservatorship there are seven powers that the conservator can obtain, and the same seven civil and legal rights of the conservatee can be limited. These powers/rights include:

1. To fix the residence or specific dwelling of the limited conservatee.
2. Access to the confidential records and papers of the limited conservatee.
3. To consent or withhold consent to the marriage of, or the entrance into a registered domestic partnership by the limited conservatee.
4. The right of the limited conservatee to contract.
5. The power of the limited conservatee to give or withhold medical consent.
6. The limited conservatee's right to control his or her own social and sexual contact and relationships.
7. Decisions concerning the education of the limited conservatee.

In this type of Conservatorship, you would get to choose which powers you want to ask the court for and which civil and legal rights of your child's you would like to limit. This Conservatorship was designed with the idea that every person with a disability has different abilities and different needs and therefore they should not all be limited in the same ways. For each of the powers, the standard for the court to grant the power is based on whether or not your child can make decisions in each of these areas as a reasonable prudent person of the same age. This Conservatorship does not need to be renewed and will be in effect until either (1) all of the Conservators pass away; (2) the Conservatee passes away; or (3) a court order terminates the Conservatorship.

The second type of Probate Conservatorship in the State of California is a General Conservatorship. This type of conservatorship is used for every other person who is unable to properly provide for his or her personal needs for physical health, food, clothing, or shelter, for reasons such as dementia or Alzheimer's. This type of Conservatorship may be used for people with mental health issues or for people with developmental disabilities as well. The Conservator in this type of conservatorship will obtain authority over housing and medical decisions and basic care, custody and control.

Which type of Conservatorship you require will be based on what authority you are seeking. Most people who have a child with developmental disabilities are best served by the Limited Conservatorship.

Probate Conservatorship law varies from state to state. Please check with a local attorney in your home state with experience with Developmental Disabilities to see what options are available to you.

Q: What is the best way to protect my adult child after I'm gone? I want him to continue to live an independent lifestyle, the same way he does now. He has epilepsy and experiences tonic-clonic seizures. Can the court step in if they feel he is at risk? Can I avoid this by writing a letter or with some type of legal document?

A: The best way to protect your child after you have passed away is to have someone ready to advocate on your child's behalf. If your child is conserved, his or her conservator will decide where he or she will reside. A Conservatorship is considered a protective proceeding. The court can always step in if there are concerns for your child's well-being; however, by having an advocate like a conservator, it is less likely that the court will get involved if there are issues. The court will watch what the conservator does; however, the conservator will be the one making the decisions. To help your child continue to live an independent lifestyle, make sure that there is an advocate for him or her, and funds to pay for his or her lifestyle. This is done through the Conservatorship and the Special Needs Trust.

Q: Can I hire a Special Needs Attorney if they practice in another state from where I live? Are the laws different from state to state?
A: Hiring an out-of-state attorney may be an option, depending on what legal work you are seeking to complete. Conservatorship law varies from state to state and you will need an attorney in your state in order to complete one. Special Needs Trusts are subject to Federal Law, so the state in which the Trustee resides is the jurisdiction of the Trust. If you are doing a Court Ordered Special Needs Trust, or a D-4 Trust for proceeds your child has already obtained, you will need an attorney in your state to assist you.

Q: How should divorced parents proceed? Who decides on who will have the power of attorney, etc.?
A: Divorced parents who have a child with disabilities can be a difficult problem. The Conservatorship can be set up in such a way that the parents are both in charge. A third person can be considered the "tie-breaker" should a disagreement ensue between them regarding their child's care. The Conservatorship can also be established so that one parent is the conservator, but the other gets some power, notification of changes in their child's life and visitation.

Regarding the Special Needs Trust, I have worked with divorced parents who do their estate plans (Living Trust, Wills, Powers of Attorney, etc.) with different attorneys and use my services to assist them with the Special Needs Trust only. Each parent can leave money to the Special Needs Trust from a personal Estate Plan and appoint a neutral trustee for the Special Needs Trust that both parties are comfortable with. In the unfortunate situations where the courts decide custody and assets, it is best that each party form their own Estate Plan.

Q: My teen-age child is profoundly disabled. He does not talk and still wears diapers. There will come a time when I will not be able to care for him. What kind of arrangements should I make?

A: Every parent who has a profoundly disabled child comes to a point where they are no longer able to care for their child. Your personal situation will dictate what arrangements you will need to make. Some families opt to place their child in a skilled nursing facility or a group home, while others pay for caregivers to come into their home and provide the care they are no longer able to provide. Other families have siblings or other close family members who are willing to take over the care when the parents are no longer able to. If you are looking at supported living for your child in the future, it is important to get your plan into your child's Individual Program Plan (IPP), so that a Regional Center can assist with the funding and help provide vendors.

The arrangements you make for your child will depend on your desires for care and your financial ability to provide for that care.

Q: If my child falls in the middle of the spectrum what would you recommend that I do?

A: No matter where you child is on the spectrum, you are the best person to decide what is best for your child. Planning for your child's future is important, and you should make sure that your plan fits your child's abilities and that you are comfortable with it. Most children in the middle of the spectrum require assistance.

A Conservatorship may be warranted, and a Special Needs Trust that will provide for your child's care after you are no longer able to can be a great tool to meet your planned future goals. If you desire your child to continue to reside in your home after you pass away, you will need to plan for caregivers to come in and assist your child, financially plan to pay for caregivers and for the upkeep, maintenance, repairs, taxes and insurance on the home.

If your desire is for your child to reside in a group home, it is important to make sure your child has an advocate to make sure that he or she is properly cared for. The Special Needs Trust can then be used for your child to go on special outings with other family members or for your child's hobbies. When your child is in the middle of the spectrum, you have more options in the care of your child after you pass away, so planning becomes crucial so that your child has the quality of life that you desire for his or her future.

In summary, The Conservatorship, Power of Attorney, Letter of Intent, and Special Needs Trust are all tools at your disposal to help you plan for your child's future. Each can be used to build a portion of the life you want for your child. The Conservatorship or Power of Attorney is the tool that is used to determine who makes legal decisions for your child, such as where your son or daughter is to live and the medical treatment he or she gets. The Special Needs Trust is a tool used to pay for all of your child's future needs. The Letter of Intent is a tool to communicate with your child's future caregivers about what they need to know about your child. When these tools are used together, you have the ability to build a solid foundation for your child's disabilities, no matter at what level they are functioning.

Now let me introduce you to Mary Anne Ehlert, a Certified Financial Planner and founder and President of Protected Tomorrows, an advocacy organization for special needs children and adults which her sister with cerebral palsy inspired her to create. I asked Mary Anne to explain basic information about various government benefits and trust options.

MAKING SENSE OF SPECIAL NEEDS PLANNING

If you are a parent of a child with special needs, government benefits and legal options are often confusing. Many parents tell us that their child is not eligible for benefits, or that everyone is turned down the first time they apply. We also hear that in order for a person with a disability to receive benefits, the parents must disinherit the child in their will. These assumptions are not true.

Here is a brief explanation of government benefits that your child may or may not be eligible for, but which you may want to investigate:

1. **SSI–Supplemental Security Income. A Federal income supplement program** funded by general tax revenues (*not* Social Security taxes). Its purpose is to financially assist the aged, blind and disabled who have little or no income, and is generally offered to people who have little or no work history. The funds it provides are to be used for basic

needs such as food, clothing and shelter. To qualify for this benefit, an applicant must limit their assets; the allowable assets include a home, one car, a pre-paid funeral, and $2,000.

2. **SSDI–Social Security Disability Insurance. A federal cash benefit program** that pays benefits to an eligible individual and certain members of his or her family. To qualify for SSDI you must be "insured;" that is, you would need to have worked a minimum length of time and paid Social Security taxes. Each insured individual should receive a statement from Social Security explaining their status of eligibility. Social Security statements can also be obtained from http://www.ssa.gov/mystatement/.

3. **Medicare–A federal health insurance program** for people 65 years of age and older, certain younger people with disabilities, and people with End-Stage Renal Disease (permanent kidney failure with dialysis or a transplant). Medicare does not cover everything, and it does not pay the total cost for most services or supplies that are covered.

4. **Medicaid–A state-run medical assistance program** for certain individuals and families with low incomes and resources, which is limited to individuals who fall into specific categories. Although the federal government establishes general guidelines for the program, the Medicaid program eligibility requirements are actually established by each state. In addition to paying for some medical services and prescriptions, Medicaid may also pay for residential facilities, workshops and other programs. The program's asset limitations are similar to those of the SSI.

It is important to create a life plan for your child. This involves understanding your vision for your child's future, and recognizing your fears as well. The next step is to identify how your vision can be made into reality and how your fears can be mitigated as you build your plan.

Although you may be dealing with an underage child at this time, what do you see for him/her in the future? Supported employment? Workshop-type employment? Residential living?

Does your existing health insurance remain in effect when your child turns 26 or is no longer a full-time student?

What assets are presently in your child's name? Example: savings bonds, life insurance, stocks, mutual funds, a home, etc.

Is there a possibility your child may inherit any money or assets? Parents often ask if there is a way to leave an inheritance to their child without negatively impacting his/her benefits. An individual may set up a Special Needs Trust that will permit this. The following are the most common types of Special Needs Trusts:

Third Party Discretionary Supplemental Needs Trust – *A trust that can hold cash, personal property, or real property, or can be the beneficiary of life insurance proceeds.* <u>Other people's money</u> or property that has been given or left to a child can be set aside safely to provide for the child's future supplemental care. There are some very specific rules for this type of trust: It must be irrevocable, the funds must be used for supplemental care only, and the trust's assets cannot be made payable to the individual with disabilities.

First Party Discretionary Supplemental Care Trust or Payback Trust – *A trust that can hold cash, personal property or real property that is <u>owned by the person</u> with disabilities.* This can *only* be set up by a person's parents, grandparents, legal guardian(s), or the court. This trust also has very specific rules and it differs from the Third Party trust in that it must have a *payback provision*. The state is reimbursed for medical expenses paid at the death of the beneficiary.

Another area to discuss is your child's future guardian(s), or Future Care People™ as we call them. Who will be there to step into your shoes if something were to happen to you? Who will handle the medical, school, employment, residential, and recreation decisions? This is one of the most important areas to document.

Last but not least, be sure to document your child's life. Think of all of the things that are specific to your child. Who else knows what you know? If something should happen to you, who will have the "instruction book" of care? Would they know never to administer a certain medication, or that a certain shampoo will give your child a horrible rash? Would they know your child's daily routines that may seem inconsequential, but are critical to your child's everyday functioning?

The Instructional Care Manual that Amalia has created is the ideal place to record this information. Be sure to review and update it regularly. While this task may appear to be just one more thing to do, in the long run, it's well worth the effort.

To many families these issues are often confusing and just plain daunting. The important thing is to be patient and do your homework so that you are better prepared for the future. There are many Internet resources available to help you, such as: www.protectedtomorrows.com, www.ssa.gov, and www.statehealthfacts.org. Protected Tomorrows also has a cost effective program of tools and resources for planning your loved one's future. (See Appendix for a special discount promo code).

Bart Stevens is a Certified Special Needs Planner who gave me permission to reprint the following story he wrote about one of his clients. The message rings out loud and clear.

BUBBA, BUBBA, BUBBA

Michael is 42 years-old and lives with his mother, Anne. Michael has multiple disabilities. His communication and functioning skills are at the level of a two-year-old. He uses a wheelchair and requires assistance for all of his needs. Anne has cared for him his entire life.

Michael is able to speak a few words. One of the things he does is roll his head from side-to-side, smile and say, "Bubba, Bubba, Bubba." I asked Anne what Michael meant. "What do you think it means?" she responded. I told her I had no idea. Anne said, "Bubba, Bubba, Bubba means 'bubbles'!" I assumed Michael wanted Anne to blow bubbles for him. But Anne explained, "It's bubbles in a soft drink. He likes the tickle in his throat when he drinks it."

This touching experience made me think, "What would happen, as in Anne's case, if you had done no planning?" The reality of mortality is that your child may very well survive you. You will not be gone for "just a few hours." You are gone permanently.

As in Michael's situation, what if there were no written information or instructions for your loved one? Imagine if Michael came to live with you, and you had to figure everything out yourself. You watch him roll his head and hear him say, "Bubba, Bubba, Bubba" a few times each day. What would you think he meant? After a few days he says it again, this time without a smile and fewer times each day. By the end of two weeks, he never says it again.

Michael's limited communication skills allowed him to express a desire for one of the few things that made him happy and gave him pleasure. Who knows what self-esteem he felt because he was able to make a request and have it understood and fulfilled. What a tragedy it would be if Anne died and never let anyone know about "Bubba, Bubba, Bubba." Think about how well and secure Michael would feel, if after losing his mother, being moved from his home, and changing his life completely, he says to his new care providers, "Bubba, Bubba, Bubba," and they know to give him that favorite soft drink.

My intention in sharing this is to help you appreciate and understand how dire the consequences will be for your loved one with special needs if you have not done any future planning for them.

This story makes it abundantly clear that the person you are hurting by not planning is your loved one with special needs. Who better than you knows and understands their wants and needs? They are relying on you to take care of them, because they cannot take partial or full care of themselves.

Planning today will eliminate your concerns so you can be assured that your loved one with special needs will have the best care, security, and quality of life possible.

TERMINOLOGY SIMPLIFIED

Legal terminology is often unfamiliar and difficult to understand. Clients frequently ask me to explain legal terms and procedures in simple layman's language. Here are a few with which every parent should be familiar:

1. Getting a Document Notarized

For a document to be notarized you must sign it in the presence of a Notary Public or court clerk. After witnessing your signature, the notary/clerk will also sign the document and then apply an official stamp. You will need to have proper identification with you, such as a driver's license or passport.

2. Letter of Intent

A Letter of Intent is a document that you prepare to help your networkers, guardians, trustees and the courts interpret your wishes for your child. It is not a formal or "legal" document, but the courts will look to it as a guide to understanding your child and your wishes. The courts tend to favor the family's wishes as long as they are not illegal or immoral.

Place your Letter of Intent in the Final Instructional Care Manual along with all your other important legal and personal documents concerning your special needs child. Be sure it contains a description of your child's disabilities and medical history, including all medications and dietary needs. A list of key contacts, educational details, and schedule of therapy and other services should also be included—the more personal the better.

3. When Is the Best Time to Begin the Guardianship Process?

If you want to create a guardianship for a child who is over the age of eighteen, you can begin the process at any time. If your child is approaching eighteen, you may start the process 2-3 months before his/her 18th birthday. It is not true that parents must seek guardianship before their child turns eighteen.

4. Choosing a Guardian/Guardianship

I believe that having an abundance of people to help out is never a problem, but having no one at all truly is.

If you know that your adult child will need a guardian, I suggest that you include your guardian(s) on your list of networkers in the Final Instructional Care Manual. I personally do not feel good about having only one guardian designated for Brandon. What if something happens to the guardian after I'm gone, and I have failed to name someone to supersede them? The courts will automatically take over and appoint a public guardian or a professional conservator. I would much prefer to have a list of networkers whom I know and trust who would be willing to step into that position, or who could help select a new guardian or conservator, rather than have the court appoint a "stranger." Your networkers can also ensure that the Final Instructional Care Manual accompanies your child for the rest of his/her life.

Here are some important questions to ask yourself when you are selecting a guardian for your child.

Does the potential guardian:
- Have a good relationship with my child? Is he/she patient, kind and compassionate?
- Know how to care for my child, or is willing to learn?

- Have the interpersonal and communication skills that will enable him/her to be an effective advocate for my child?
- Have enough time and energy to devote to my child?

If you answered yes to all the questions, it is likely you have found a good candidate. If you answered no to any of them, you will need to look further. Once you feel you have found a good match, talk openly with your potential guardian about the responsibilities involved. Be sure to periodically review your choice of guardian. Keep in mind that your child's needs may change, or at some point the person may become unable or unwilling to assume the role for the long term.

5. A Last Will and Testament

I cannot emphasize enough that every parent of a special needs child needs to have a proper will drawn up. A will is considered the cornerstone of an effective estate plan. If you own a home, a car, have a checking and/or savings account, you have an estate and you need to have a will. A will ensures that the disposition of your property will be according to your wishes.

I know how this area can stir up negative emotions for many parents, myself included. It is a great sign that you were willing to read this chapter. However, after reading this information if you still feel overwhelmed I suggest you give it some time to digest. I have had to do that myself over the years and I have found when I do take a break I am able to return with more courage, gusto, and the willingness to tackle this daunting task. I believe in time you will be able to face it just like everything else, one-step at a time. You must be kind to yourself just as you are to your children. You cannot be pushed, just as you would not push your children, and I believe that at your own pace and time you will be able to master it all.

I am here to cheer you on and support you as we walk hand-in-hand, traveling this path into the unknown future together.

Notes

Notes

Epilogue

I Never Expected This to Happen So Quickly

*We make a living by what we get,
but we make a life by what we give.*

Winston Churchill

After speaking on the theme of this book at a conference recently, a mother told me that she wished she could live just one day longer than her disabled child. Her comment struck me deeply. Although I understood where she was coming from, and that every parent of a special needs child would find this the "ideal" scenario, it likely would not occur this way for most of us. We need to face the reality that our child will probably outlive us, and we must have plans in place for our child's care. The conversation I had with that dear mother made me *all the more determined to make sure Brandon's Final Instructional Care Manual was complete and up to date.*

Beginning the process took courage and plenty of it. I knew it was unwise to delay, and when Brandon turned forty, the time felt right. However, staring my own mortality in the face was extremely difficult for me; the reality that my passing was inevitable was discomforting and brought on waves of sadness. I'm a "take charge" kind of gal and known for tackling things head on, so I was surprised at how often I had to grit my teeth and fight a deep desire to procrastinate.

However, after I filled out the manual and began to select my networkers, I asked a few of them if they would be willing to start working with Brandon right away. I decided there was no need to wait.

At the exact same time, Brandon received a call from an Independent Living Service (ILS) agency. The owner of the agency told him that she had a counselor who could start right away. What great timing, I thought. Although his new counselor would not be considered a networker, I decided to treat her as such for the time being. One of the reasons she could not be a networker is that we have little to no control over who our child gets from these agencies. Another is that she is not volunteering; she is getting paid. However, these service providers can be a beneficial addition to your helpers even if they do not meet the networker criteria.

For example, Joe, Brandon's first Independent Living Counselor through the Regional Center, was excellent. He owned an ILS agency and worked with my son for six years. Without his guidance and support it would have been nearly impossible for Brandon to succeed when he initially embarked on his journey to independence.

I soon discovered that starting to integrate new people into Brandon's life now was a good idea, as he was having difficulty expressing himself clearly to his new Independent Living Counselor. Rather than interfere, I chose to step back and observe how they worked things out between them. I visited less frequently and mostly offered help over the phone when asked. Brandon told me that she was teaching him how to prepare food, but said, "She thinks I am a chef. This is just too much work for me." We both laughed, but I understood exactly what the issue was. *Often when helpers first meet my son, they do not recognize his limitations and tend to expect too much from him.* He asked me to send her an email for him, to explain the difficulty he was having communicating, which I did. She then realized that Brandon needed to start off slowly when being introduced to anything new, and thankfully she was flexible and willing to adapt her teaching methods to his learning style. Brandon was working with her four hours a week and was making great strides. He seemed to like her and told me he wanted to "try new things and add fun things to do together."

Observing their interaction from a distance was a wonderful eye opener. Although I was fully aware of Brandon's difficulty with communication, I realized the information in his Instructional Care Manual was not adequate and had to be rewritten and also simplified. *How else would I have known this area needed clarification if I hadn't taken the opportunity to test it while I still had the chance?*

Unfortunately, his work with this counselor came to an abrupt end when he found out that the agency's policy required two counselors to be present when a client with epilepsy was taken out into the community. He called me, clearly upset. "I feel like I am being treated like a child and my independence is being taken away from me," he said.

In all the years my son has been on his own, he has never had any service provider require two people to accompany him when he goes out. I checked with the Epilepsy Foundation to see if this was a new protocol, and they said no, it must be the agency's own policy.

The agency also attempted to monitor Brandon's seizure medication, and alleged that he was not taking it properly, which was not true. Brandon endured this for two months before he texted his counselor and told her not to return. He wrote, "Don't come tomorrow. I'm done."

A week later, she called Brandon to see if he would change his mind, but he told her plainly over the phone, "I want to be alone, and I don't want you to come back."

Afterwards, Brandon phoned me. "I just wanted a friend, someone I could talk to and do fun things with, but that never happened," he said. Although I was saddened that he was no longer going to be working with a counselor, I was amazed and impressed that Brandon was able to speak up for himself so forthrightly. Speaking his mind is something he could never do, except with me, so you can imagine how proud I was of my son. Although this counselor did not work out, Brandon gained something far more precious—his voice. *You just never know when your child will turn a negative situation into a learning and growing experience.*

I used to be afraid that Brandon would not fare well on his own after I'm gone but that fear and worry have all but vanished. This new level of trust I have took me completely by surprise. I attribute my newfound feelings of strength and resolve to having created an Instructional Care Manual for my son, and to experiences like the one I just shared which helped to reinforce my confidence in Brandon's future.

I wanted to share this information with you because I feel the sooner you acquire networkers and have them start working with your child, the better off you and your child will be. You will see where the strengths and weaknesses of your care plan are, and you can make adjustments and improvements to it while you have the chance, *now*. You will develop successful strategies for handling "time and chance" circumstances. It will be too late to work these things out and modify your manual when you are no longer here. I guarantee that the more accurate and thorough you can make your manual, the more peace you will have about your child's future.

Today, I am optimistic about my son's future and how he will fare after I'm gone. I know he will do just fine. This is the first time I have been able to say this openly and truly believe it. I have come a long way and have done my work, and I know that you will, too. While I am here I can assist Brandon's networkers when necessary to help them work more effectively with my son. Brandon is also learning what he can do to help others understand him better.

I never expected this to happen so quickly. I am grateful to be able to watch it all come together in real time with real people while I am still here. This gives me tremendous hope.

The Working Manual in this book is for you to have space to write everything you need to communicate about your child. When you are ready to transfer this information to the Final Instructional Care Manual you will be able to download it from my website at www.AmaliaStarr.com. You will have the ability to change it or refine it to best suit you and your child's needs. You can add, subtract, shorten, lengthen, and change the item order. *Because of this manual your voice, wishes and desires will live on long after you're gone.* Just remember to be clear in your writing, wise in your selection process, and continue to update your information periodically.

I hope after reading this book *you know that you no longer have to live in fear of the future.* By getting your networkers on board and taking action now you are sure to feel as empowered as I do. This is the goal that I wish for you and have faith that you will achieve.

Appendix

Autism Society

The Autism Society strives to provide Information and Referral (I&R) through one-to-one interaction with an I&R specialist. Thousands of people turn to their website for valuable information (www.autism-society.org), which includes a comprehensive database of resources called Autism Source™. These resources encompass federal, state and local government agencies; professionals; service providers; support systems; medical and educational providers; research facilities, and more.

Autism Society of America (ASA)

7910 Woodmont Avenue, Suite 300
Bethesda, MD 20814-3067
Phone: (301) 657-0881 or (800) 328-8476
Website: www.autism-society.org

Best Buddies California

The mission of Best Buddies is to enhance the lives of people with intellectual disabilities by providing opportunities for one-to-one friendships and employment.

Best Buddies
5601 West Slauson Avenue, #255
Culver City, CA 90230
Phone: (310) 642-2620
Fax: (310) 642-2630
Website: www.bestbuddiescalifornia.org

The B.E.S.T. Technique

Gina De Masi
2001 Barrington Avenue, Suite 308
Los Angeles, CA 90025
(310) 829-6829

The Bio Energetic Synchronization Technique (B.E.S.T.) is a physical, yet non-forceful energy balancing procedure using the hands to reestablish the full natural healing potential of the body. B.E.S.T. removes the interference and/or distractions that are demanding the attention of the body's healing power. This interference causes an imbalance in the autonomic nervous system, and ultimately leads to disease.
To locate a B.E.S.T practitioner in your area contact:

Morter Health System
215 West Poplar
Rogers, AK 72756
(800) 874-1478
Website: www.morter.com

California Department of Developmental Services (DDS)
(Regional Centers)

The California Department of Developmental Services is the agency through which the State of California provides services and support to individuals with developmental disabilities. These include intellectual disabilities, cerebral palsy, epilepsy, autism and related conditions. Services are provided through state-operated developmental centers and community facilities, and contracts with 21 nonprofit regional centers. The regional centers serve as a local resource to help find and access the services and support available to individuals with developmental disabilities and their families.

California Department of Developmental Services
1600 9th Street
P. O. Box 944202
Sacramento, CA 94244-2020
Info: (916) 654-1690
TTY: (916) 654-2054

Easter Seals

For more than ninety years, Easter Seals has provided education, outreach and advocacy services to help people living with autism and other disabilities address life's challenges and achieve personal goals. From child development centers to physical rehabilitation and job training, Easter Seals offers a variety of services to help individuals with disabilities to live, learn, work and play in our communities.

Easter Seals
233 South Wacker Drive, Suite 2400
Chicago, IL 60606
800-221-6827 (toll-free)
Website: www.easterseals.com

Seizure First Aid - Epilepsy Foundation

Generalized tonic-clonic seizures are the ones which most people generally think of when they hear the word "epilepsy." During a seizure, a person may fall to the ground, remain unconscious, or have involuntary spasms. Most seizures last a few seconds or minutes, and end naturally.

What to Do:
Cushion the person's head. Remove eyeglasses and loosen tight clothing (such as a tie or scarf). Turn the person on his/her side, and provide ample space. Do not restrain the person. Do not put anything in his/her mouth. Remain calm, and time how long the seizures last. Look for ID indicating epilepsy

or other medical condition. Most seizures do not require emergency medical attention.

Call a Doctor or 911 When:
A seizure lasts more than five minutes, and the person:
- Is pregnant
- Does not regain consciousness
- Does not breathe after one minute
- Has one seizure after another
- Is injured
- Asks for help
- Has no medical ID

Simplefill

Established in 2009, Simplefill is an advocacy team committed to helping uninsured and underinsured low-income Americans afford their brand-name medicines. The program helps hundreds of patients each month obtain their prescriptions for a fraction of their out-of-pocket costs.

Currently, the monthly service fees vary from $50-$85, and are based on the number of medications prescribed. Medications will either come directly to your home, to your doctor's office, or they can be picked up from your local pharmacy. You can cancel at any time. They do not hold patients to any contract. For more information, call (1-877) 386-0206 or email: questions@simplefill.com.

The Special Needs Alliance

The Special Needs Alliance (SNA) is a non-profit organization that was formed in 2002 by a group of prominent, credentialed disability and elder law attorneys who recognized the unique planning needs of younger individuals with disabilities and their families. It currently has members in 47 states. (www.SpecialNeedsAlliance.org). The mission of the SNA is to maintain and make available a professional organization of attorneys skilled in the complex areas of public entitlements, estate, trust and tax planning, and legal issues involving individuals with physical and cognitive disabilities.

SNA attorneys can determine availability of state and federal benefits, protect public benefits eligibility, establish Special Needs Trusts, and manage Trust benefits. Their services include:
- Drafting Special Needs Trusts
- Drafting Special Needs Wills
- Estate Planning
- Financial Planning & Legal Assistance for Disabled Persons
- Living Trusts
- Conservatorship
- Guardianship
- Personal Injury and Medical Malpractice Settlements
- Preparation of Trust Accountings
- Structured Settlement Negotiations
- Trust Distributions

Vocational Independence Program (VIP)

This is a practical college program for students with learning disabilities. The curriculum is competency based and students are placed in classes according to their ability in each individual area. VIP is divided into four major areas: Academics, Social Development, Vocational Skills, and Independent Living.

Vocational Independence Program
New York Institute of Technology
Central Islip Campus
P.O. Box 9029
Central Islip, NY 11722
Phone: 800-345-6948
Website: www.nyit.edu

About the Contributing Writers

Christopher A. Poulos is an attorney who has an adult son with cerebral palsy and developmental delay. His law practice focuses on individuals with special needs and includes Guardianship, Conservatorships and Probate, Regional Center Appeals, and Estate Planning. Christopher is considered an expert on Special Needs Trusts. He is a popular speaker and has served on the Board of Directors of several non-profit organizations that focus on the care and rights of persons with developmental disabilities and their families.
101 N. Orange Ave., Suite C
West Covina, CA 91790
Phone: (626) 960-9373 Fax (626) 960-9924
Website: www.specialneedslawfirm.com Email: capouloslaw@aol.com

Mary Anne Ehlert is a Certified Financial Planner and the founder and President of Protected Tomorrows, Inc., an organization dedicated to enhancing the lives of families with members who have special needs. Protected Tomorrows addresses such issues as planning future care funding, government benefits, residential options, employment opportunities, recreational choices, education options and family dynamics.
Readers may obtain a 10% discount on the Family Membership Online System with this promo code (case sensitive): **EHLERT_CARE**
Protected Tomorrows, Inc.
103 Schelter Rd. Lincolnshire, IL 60069
Phone: (847) 522-8086 Fax: (847) 522-8081
Website: www.protectedtomorrows.com Email: info@protectedtomorrows.com

Bart Stevens is the author of ABC's *Special Needs Planning Made Easy* and *The Special Needs Education and Advocacy Project,* a non-profit dedicated to helping families provide for the care and security of their loved ones with special needs.
Bart Stevens Special Needs Planning, LLC
4121 E. Palo Brea Lane
Cave Creek, Arizona 85331
Phone: (480) 991-0909 Toll Free: (888) 447-2525 Fax: (480) 556-0714
www.bssnp.com

About the Author

Amalia Starr is a motivational speaker, transition and independent living coach, founder of Autism Independence Project, and mother to an autistic adult son. She is the author of *Raising Brandon: Creating a Path to Independence for Your Adult "Kid" with Autism & Special Needs.* In it she describes how she led her son Brandon to independence when the professionals deemed it impossible.

As the founder of the Autism Independence Project, she invented a program she named the *Step-In Parenting Network (SIPN).* This program is set up to screen, educate, and teach those who are willing to step into the role of a substitute parent when a special needs child's parents have passed away or when they are unable to care for their son or daughter due to illness or aging.

Amalia offers keynotes, presentations, and conducts workshops and coaching sessions worldwide. With more than forty years of experience, she specializes in independence training for parents, teaching them how to help their special needs children reach their full potential and gain maximum independence. She has been recognized as a pioneer and trailblazer.

Amalia's clients have benefited greatly from her private consulting and training sessions. Because every child is unique, she works with parents to create a personalized program for their children. This can include strategies for independence, possible work placement, housing alternatives, and other options.

Amalia's mission is to support and teach parents how to help their autistic and special needs children cross over to independence and to ensure that they are well taken care of after their parents are gone.

To contact Amalia for keynotes, presentations, seminars, workshops and private consultations:

Amalia@AmaliaStarr.com
www.AmaliaStarr.com
Twitter: @AutismMomExpert
Toll Free: (800) 939-1046
Private sessions can also be conducted over Skype.

Your Working Instructional Care Manual

This working manual is where you will begin preparing all the personal and crucial information about your special needs child for those who will step in for you after you are gone. Because of this manual your voice, wishes and desires will live on for years to come. Just remember to be clear in your writing and continue to update your information periodically. Since this is a work in progress extra pages will be included; there are more note pages in the back of the book for making updates as needed.

Your Child's Full Name _____

Nickname _____

Birthdate _____

Parent's Signature _____

Date _____

Contents

Your Working Instructional Care Manual

Section 1. Personal: Important Information About My Child
1. Letter of Intent
2. My Child's Diagnosis
3. Brief Description of My Child in a Paragraph (300 words or less) and in a List
4. Photo Page
5. The Most Important Thing You Must Know About My Child
6. My Child's "Gray" Areas, Which Would Not Be Apparent Unless I Told You
7. A List of Tidbits
8. Schedules and Routines
9. Must Have and Cannot Have
10. Likes and Dislikes
11. Favorite Things
12. What Makes My Child Angry, Sad, Frustrated, Upset or Scared
13. What Soothes and Gives My Child Pleasure
14. What Not to Do and Where My Child Cannot Go
15. Write Helpful Teaching Stories and Q&A
16. Summary and Overview List

Section 2. Additional Pertinent Information

- **Emergency Contact Information and Medical Care:** Physicians, Dentists, Therapists, Pharmacies, Medications, Health Conditions, Allergies, and First Aid Procedures

- **Special Dietary Needs, Meals and Food:** Dietary Restrictions and Favorite Foods

- **Legal Matters:** Attorneys, Financial Advisors, Insurance Information, etc.

- **Family Background:** Past and Present

- **School and Education:** Past, Present, and Future

- **Employment:** Past, Present, and Future

- **Residential:** Past, Present, and Future

- **Social Activities/Recreation:** Likes and Dislikes

- **Religious Affiliation:** Past, Present, and Future

- **Making Final Arrangements:** Be Prepared

- **Summary and Overview List**

Before you Begin

When it comes to describing your child, the more detailed the better. Feel free to answer as many of the questions in the working manual that pertain to your child, and of course you can add any of your own. I wanted to make it user friendly and inviting to encourage you to write anything that comes to mind. Feel free to adapt or use what I wrote in the Sample Manual in Chapter Four if it applies to your child. There will be additional blank pages for you to add whatever you wish. This is designed to help you corral all of your information in one place until you are ready to transfer it into the Final Instructional Care Manual. I will talk more about that towards the end of this chapter.

Your Introductory Letter of Intent

Remember, in the Final ICM you will be able to personalize a "generic" letter by simply adding a networker's name, or you may wish to write a more in-depth letter that is meant for someone specific. If you like, you can refer to my Letter of Intent in Chapter Four and use it as a guide.

Your Working Instructional Care Manual

My Letter of Intent

My Child's Diagnosis

(in a few sentences)

It is imperative that your networkers know what your child's diagnosis is. You can write just a line or two as I did in the Sample Manual or as much as you wish, as this information is sure to appear throughout the manual again and again.

Your Working Instructional Care Manual

A Brief Description of My Child

(300 words or less)

A Short List About My Child

Although it says "a short list", there is extra space to write and rewrite if you wish.

1. _____
2. _____
3. _____
4. _____
5. _____
6. _____
7. _____
8. _____
9. _____
10. _____
11. _____
12. _____
13. _____
14. _____
15. _____
16. _____
17. _____
18. _____

Your Working Instructional Care Manual

Notes

Photograph Page

Attach you family photos here and have fun with it! Be creative and feel free to express yourself through pictures.

Your Working Instructional Care Manual

The Most Important Thing You Must Know About My Child

My Child's Gray Areas, Which Would Not Be Apparent Unless I Told You

A List of "Tidbits"—Small Pieces of Interesting Information About My Child

1. _____
2. _____
3. _____
4. _____
5. _____
6. _____
7. _____
8. _____
9. _____
10. _____
11. _____
12. _____
13. _____
14. _____
15. _____
16. _____
17. _____
18. _____
19. _____

My Child's Schedules and Routines

Your Working Instructional Care Manual

What My Child Must Have and Cannot Have

My Child's Likes and Dislikes

Your Working Instructional Care Manual

My Child's Favorite Things

1. Color _____

2. Music _____

3. Toy _____

4. Stuffed Animal _____

5. Food _____

6. Game _____

7. Book _____

8. TV Show _____

9. Movie _____

10. Electronics _____

11. Art _____

12. Clothes _____

13. Person _____

14. Animal _____

15. _____

16. _____

17. _____

What Makes My Child Angry, Sad, Frustrated, Upset, or Scared

Your Working Instructional Care Manual

What Soothes and Gives My Child Pleasure

What Not To Do and Where My Child Cannot Go

Your Working Instructional Care Manual

Helpful Teaching Stories and Questions & Answers

(see Chapter Six for suggestions)

Section 1: Summary and Overview List

Make a list, beginning with the most important information you want your networkers to know. This summary and overview must capture the essence of your child's needs in a single page or two. I was able to select my information by simply looking through Section 1 and choosing one piece at a time.

1. _____
2. _____
3. _____
4. _____
5. _____
6. _____
7. _____
8. _____
9. _____
10. _____
11. _____
12. _____
13. _____
14. _____
15. _____
16. _____
17. _____

Your Working Instructional Care Manual

18. _____
19. _____
20. _____
21. _____
22. _____
23. _____
24. _____
25. _____
26. _____
27. _____
28. _____
29. _____
30. _____
31. _____
32. _____
33. _____
34. _____
35. _____
36. _____
37. _____
38. _____

Section 2. Additional Pertinent Information:

- **Emergency Contact Information and Medical Care:** Physicians, Dentists, Therapists, Pharmacies, Medications, Health Conditions, Allergies, and First Aid Procedures

- **Special Dietary Needs, Meals and Food:** Dietary Restrictions and Favorite Foods

- **Legal Matters:** Attorneys, Financial Advisors, Insurance Information, etc.

- **Family Background:** Past and Present

- **School and Education:** Past, Present, and Future

- **Employment:** Past, Present, and Future

- **Residential:** Past, Present, and Future

- **Social Activities/Recreation:** Likes and Dislikes

- **Religious Affiliation:** Past, Present, and Future

- **Making Final Arrangements:** Be Prepared

- **Summary and Overview List**

Your Working Instructional Care Manual

EMERGENCY CONTACT INFORMATION

Name						Relationship					Email						Phone

_____

_____

_____

_____

_____

_____

_____

_____

Notes _____

_____

_____

_____

I Have Autism...What'll I Do Without You, Mom?

Physicians, Dentists, Therapists, Pharmacies

    Name   Relationship   Email   Phone

1. _____
2. _____
3. _____
4. _____
5. _____
6. _____
7. _____
8. _____
9. _____
10. _____
11. _____
12. _____
13. _____
14. _____
15. _____
16. _____
17. _____
18. _____

Your Working Instructional Care Manual

Notes

Medications, Health Conditions, and Allergies

1. _____
2. _____
3. _____
4. _____
5. _____
6. _____
7. _____
8. _____
9. _____
10. _____
11. _____
12. _____
13. _____
14. _____
15. _____

Notes _____
_____
_____
_____

Your Working Instructional Care Manual

First Aid Procedures

Special Dietary Restrictions and Needs, Supplements, Meals, and Favorite Foods

Your Working Instructional Care Manual

Legal Matters: Financial Advisors, Attorneys, Insurance Information, etc.

	Name	Relationship	Email	Phone

1. _____
2. _____
3. _____
4. _____
5. _____
6. _____
7. _____
8. _____
9. _____
10. _____
11. _____
12. _____
13. _____
14. _____
15. _____
16. _____
17. _____
18. _____

Family Background

Write about family members your child knows and likes and those he or she does not like or does not want to be around. In addition, you can include information about your family history such as where you were born, raised, and married if you feel it is relevant.

_____

_____

_____

_____

_____

_____

_____

_____

_____

_____

School and Education

Past, Present and Future Experiences

What types of schools has your child attended? What form of education do you see in your child's future: vocational, academic, special school, mainstream classes or other?

Employment

Past, Present, and Future

Has your child worked or volunteered in the past? Does your child have something he or she likes to do that could be turned into a "real" job?

A Few Options:

- Working with a job coach or mentor.
- Working fully independently.
- Creating a special job that suits your child's ability, strength and desire.

Your Working Instructional Care Manual

Residential

Past, Present, and Future
What are your child's living experiences thus far? Where has your child lived in the past and where does he or she live today? Do you have a future living arrangement plan?

A Few Options:

- Supervised living
- Living with relatives or friends
- Group homes
- Own apartment
- Intentional Communities
  See page 146 for more options.

Social Activities/Recreation

- Is your child involved in any type of social or recreational activities?
- Are there special activities your son or daughter especially enjoys doing or being part of?

Religious Affiliation

- Does your child attend religious services? How often?
- Do you want your child to continue attending special services at a particular church or temple?
- Is there anyone associated with the church/temple that your child has a special connection with?

Making Final Arrangements

This is an important area to take care of. When Brandon was nine years old he had his first epileptic seizure. Not long after, my in-laws were making their cemetery arrangements and decided to make them for Brandon as well. They purchased everything for Brandon, and I must say at the time I did not give it much thought. However, today I feel it was a very loving, kind, and generous gesture. Because of them I no longer have to deal with this matter, which is a huge relief. If you can make these arrangements sooner rather than later I believe you, too, will feel relieved, and it will be one less thing for you to have to think about or do later on.

Section 2: Summary and Overview List

Make a list beginning with the most important information you want your helpers/ networkers to know. This summary and overview must capture the essence of your child's needs in a single page or two. I was able to select my information by simply looking through Section 2 and choosing one piece at a time.

1. _____
2. _____
3. _____
4. _____
5. _____
6. _____
7. _____
8. _____
9. _____
10. _____
11. _____
12. _____
13. _____
14. _____
15. _____
16. _____

17. _____
18. _____
19. _____
20. _____
21. _____
22. _____
23. _____
24. _____
25. _____
26. _____
27. _____
28. _____
29. _____
30. _____
31. _____
32. _____
33. _____
34. _____
35. _____
36. _____
37. _____

Notes

Some Final Words

After forty-one years on the special needs trail, I can clearly see that our special needs children are here to mold us and help us as much, if not more, than we help them. As I began this book, I too, shall end it. Brandon has been and continues to be my finest teacher.

This is for you:

- If you find yourself crying allow your tears to flow freely; they can be very healing.

- May you take each day as it comes and walk one step at a time.

- Celebrate the fact that you are doing all you can, while you can.

Always remember, it's a new day and what you do today matters most.

Until we meet again,

Amalia Starr

The Final Instructional Care Manual

Your Final Instructional Care Manual can be downloaded from my website at: www.AmaliaStarr.com. You will be able to fill it in and print it out from your computer. It will also give you extra space to write what you want and need to say. You will be able to change, add or update anything easily before you create a permanent PDF file. Make copies and keep them in a safe place with your other important documents.

Your child's history will support those you have selected to assist your child, and help them ensure that the quality and consistency of your child's life is maintained. Keep your Final Instructional Care Manual and your audios and videos up to date and all together in one place. Be sure to tell a few trustworthy people where they can find this information.

I am leaving crucial information about _____, my special needs child, in this Final Instructional Care Manual, for those who will step in to help after I'm gone or if I can no longer care for my child due to aging or illness.

Parent/Guardian Signature _____

Date _____

Parent/Guardian Signature _____

Date _____

Child's Full Name _____

Nickname _____

Birthdate _____

Document Your Information with a Camera or a Recorder

In this digital age, pictures can truly be worth a thousand words. A wonderful way to supplement the information in your ICM is to make a video of yourself answering key questions about your child.

I asked a dear friend of mine to film me while she asked me a list of questions I had prepared in advance. She had met Brandon several times and knew a lot about him which helped me feel at ease. I made several of these videos and periodically review them to see if they need updating.

An even easier way to document information is to use a voice recorder. You can do this by yourself and at your own convenience. There were times when I found myself wanting the support of a loving friend and felt that a video was the best route to go, so I chose that medium. But other times a voice recording seemed the better choice. Whichever one you choose will depend on which medium you feel will best communicate your information. You may want to do both, as I did.

You can access my video and audio recordings at www.AmaliaStarr.com and www.AutismIndependenceProject.com. The videos can also be viewed on You Tube http:/bit.ly/AmaliaSpeakerVideo.

To help you get started, ask yourself this question, "What is the most important thing I want people to know about my child?" For example: My child is often misunderstood. Qualify it by going into detail and explain what you mean by "misunderstood." He does not speak well. He has a hard time expressing himself and communicating. He laughs when things are not funny, etc.

Be open and honest, clear and concise. Make your audios and videos easy to understand. Think of what you want to get across before you begin. You may want to make a few notes or have one or two sentences prepared to help you get started; then let go and allow your authenticity to shine as you speak from the heart.

If you choose to make recordings, keep your Final Instructional Care Manual and your recordings together in one place. Review and update them periodically. *Your videos and recordings will live on for years to come.*

Notes

Notes

Notes

Notes

Notes

Notes

Notes

Notes

Notes

There is HOPE!

www.ingramcontent.com/pod-product-compliance
Lightning Source LLC
Chambersburg PA
CBHW080242170426
43192CB00014BA/2529